HIS MAJESTY
KING GEORGES
SPEECHES IN INDIA

HIS MAJESTY
KING GEORGES
SPEECHES IN INDIA

G. A. NATESAN

GYAN

Published by

GYAN

Gyan Publishing House
5, Ansari Road
Daryaganj, New Delhi-110002
Phone: 011-47034999, 9811692060
E-mail: books@gyanbooks.com

Distribution Network
gyanbooks.com
India, USA, Canada, UK, Australia

ISBN: 978-93-7225-064-0 (PB)

2nd Impression 2025

Printed at: Gyan Press, Delhi.

HIS MAJESTY KING GEORGES SPEECHES IN INDIA
Author: G. A. NATESAN

HIS MAJESTY
KING GEORGE'S
SPEECHES IN INDIA.

A COMPLETE COLLECTION OF
ALL THE SPEECHES DELIVERED IN INDIA
DURING HIS TOUR AS PRINCE OF WALES AND IN
CONNECTION WITH THE RECENT CORONATION DURBAR.

PUBLISHERS' NOTE.

This is a complete and up-to-date collection of all the speeches delivered by His Majesty the King-Emperor, during his first tour in India as Prince of Wales and his second tour in connection with the Coronation Durbar. No speech of any importance relating to India has been omitted; and to make this handy collection of His Majesty's Indian Speeches doubly valuable, a useful Appendix has been added, containing among others, the text of the announcement relating to the Coronation Durbar Boons; the Proclamations of H. M. King George, Queen Victoria and King Edward the Seventh on their accession to the throne and the messages of Queen Victoria and King Edward to the Durbars of 1877 and of 1903. The book contains a fine portrait of Their Majesties as frontispiece and seven other illustrations. The Publishers venture to hope that this handy volume will be welcomed by the millions of His Majesty's subjects not only in India but all over the British Empire.

CONTENTS.

PART I. PAGE.

CONTENTS.

PART II.

APPENDIX.

ILLUSTRATIONS.

To Face Page 1.

H. M. THE KING-EMPEROR.

H. M. THE QUEEN-EMPRESS.

H. M. KING GEORGE'S SPEECHES ON INDIA.

BOMBAY CORPORATION ADDRESS.

[His Majesty as Prince of Wales arrived on 9th November 1905, and was presented with an address by the Bombay Corporation, the same being read in clear strident tones (as Dr. Stanley Reed puts it in his account of the Royal Tour). Replying to it, His Majesty said :]

Mr. President and Gentlemen of the Municipal Corporation of Bombay,—I thank you most sincerely for the kind and enthusiastic welcome which you have given to the Princess of Wales and myself. We are both deeply moved by your touching allusion to her presence here. She is, indeed, proud to be the first Princess of Wales to have set foot on these shores. (Cheers.)

The words of your address, eloquent as they are, will not, however, convey to our fellow-subjects in other parts of the Empire what we see here to-day. Nor do they render full justice to the efforts and good-will of the citizens of this great western port of India, which culminate in this splendid ceremony.

Just thirty years ago, all but a day, my dear father, the King-Emperor, was standing not far from this very spot, and was saying that it had been the dream of his life to see India. (Loud Cheers.) The Princess and I have had similar anticipations; and we thank you from the bottom of our hearts for the manner in which you and your fellow-workers have brought these dreams to realisation. In thus following in the footsteps of my father, we are but carrying out the tradition established by him, and one which, I trust, will be repeated as generation succeeds generation. I hope, and, indeed, I am confident, that the same loving interest in this great Continent, which was inspired in my father's heart by his visit to India, and which has never abated, will equally come to us. (Cheers.)

If, as we travel through the various countries which make up this great Empire, the Princess and I can win the sympathy and good-will of the peoples of India, we shall secure a precious result from the voyage which we have been privileged to undertake. It is the last stage of our memorable and happy mission of four years ago to His

Majesty's great Dominions across the Seas. Though strangers to this beautiful city, we have read much and heard much of your trials and achievements. As the capital of Western India, and the port which links this Eastern continent with Europe, Bombay has had to adapt herself, more, perhaps, than any other Oriental city, to the requirements of modern life. She has to live up to her position, and as the threshold of this picturesque and fascinating land of India that position is somewhat exacting. But if I may judge from a brief impression from the sea, and from what I have observed here, Bombay does not fall short of her obligations. Apart from the beauty of her buildings and her natural advantages, she has thoughts for trade facilities, and for what is of equal, or, perhaps, greater importance, for the health and well-being of nearly 800,000 people.

I am delighted to be associated with the new Dock and with the first large street which the City Improvement Trust has constructed. Like all great cities which depend on commerce, Bombay has had her vicissitudes, and your Municipal history has its counterpart in many other cities of our Empire which I have had the pleasure of visiting. Your period of prosperity has endowed you with buildings and other possessions of which you may well be proud. (Cheers) But it also brought you a population, perhaps inconveniently large, and you are now wisely grappling with the problems which have beset us in the West—the problems of wide streets and healthy industrial quarters.

I wish you, Mr. Chairman, and all who are working for the welfare of Bombay, God-speed. I can imagine no nobler work than the endeavour of the individual to do something for his town.

There is one drawback to journeys such as that on which the Princess and I are now starting. Time is all too short to see everything, and to tell everyone who has joined in greeting us how heartily grateful we are. I have inherited from my father (cheers) and from our late beloved Sovereign (cheers) your first Queen-Empress, a love for India and for Indians. (Cheers). From my youth I have associated the name of India with qualities of kindness, loyalty, courtesy and bravery, and I doubt not that these early ideas will be confirmed and strengthened by the experiences which await me in the next few months. (Cheers.) We cannot, as we should like, see all your many institutions, but we hope to have opportunities of gaining some insight into those of a similar character in other parts of India. We both hope to carry home with us, not only a warm sympathy and affection for the people of India, but an increased and abiding interest in India's wants and problems, and an acquaintance with the various classes, official and non-official, British and Indian, which, under God's providence, are labouring to one end—the well-being of India and the happiness of her peoples. (Cheers.)

I will not fail to convey to the King-Emperor the expression of your loyal devotion to his Throne and person. (Cheers.) And, remembering that to-day we celebrate His Majesty's birthday, these assurances will come to him with especial gratification. (Cheers.) And I feel sure that this great company will join with me in wishing him very many happy returns of the day. (Loud and prolonged cheers.)

PRINCE OF WALES' MUSEUM, BOMBAY. LAYING FOUNDATION STONE.

[In Bombay, His Majesty laid the foundation stone of the Prince of Wales' Museum, and in replying to an address presented to him on the occasion by Sir Lawrence Jenkins, then Chief Justice of Bombay, said :—]

Sir Lawrence Jenkins,—I wish to thank all of you on behalf of the Princess of Wales and myself for the compliment which you have paid us by commemorating our visit in a manner so useful and so lasting. If we had been asked to suggest an object for your warm-hearted and generous efforts, we should have chosen an institution such as you contemplate, for we have heard of the pleasure which museums in other parts of India afford to the people. You have with justice alluded to the sympathy shown by my dear father, the King Emperor, in the educational and artistic progress of our people. It interests me to find that in this land, so strange at present to me, you are following ideas which are very familiar to us in Great Britain and throughout the Empire. Day by day we are grasping the importance of education by object lessons, and I anticipate the happiest results from the museum, library and art gallery which will one day stand upon this spot. If, as you assure us, the buildings of which I am proud to lay the foundation-stone to-day are to be fully in keeping with the other architectural adornments of this beautiful city, then we shall feel that our visit has not only brought pleasure to ourselves, but permanent advantage and happiness to the citizens of Bombay and to the thousands of strangers who visit this busy centre of commerce and Government.

To-day's ceremony is a practical proof of that public spirit of the people of Bombay about which we have so often heard. At the same time, you were fortunate to have in Lord Lamington a Governor quick to see a local want. I must also congratulate you on your Corporation, wise to recognise that a great capital like this has its intellectual as well as its material requirements; and last but by no means least, on having in your midst such citizens as your Sheriff, Mr. Sassoon J. David, and Mr. Currimbhoy Ebrahim. I hope that they and all of you who have helped to bring this public-spirited idea to fulfilment will live long to see and enjoy what, under wise and experienced direction, may prove to be one of the most important and beneficial institutions of Bombay.

AT ALEXANDRA DOCK.

[Another speech His Majesty made at Bombay was on the occasion he laid the foundation-stone of the Alexandra Dock. In replying to an address presented to him at the time, he spoke to the following effect :—]

Gentlemen,—The Princess of Wales and I are much pleased to be present here to lay the foundation-stone of this new Dock, which I understand is to be one of the largest in the world, and we heartily wish all success to the great enterprise with which we are now associated. It is a further development of the scheme so wisely initiated by Sir Seymour Fitzgerald and Lord Mayo in the constitution of a Port Trust, more than 36 years ago.

There is to us an additional satisfaction in performing this ceremony, when we remember that the King-Emperor, on the occasion of his visit to Bombay in 1875, laid the foundation-stone of your first great Dock, which has since been known as the "Prince's Dock." I congratulate the City of Bombay upon the almost unprecedented increase in her sea-borne trade since that time.

As a sailor I am especially interested to hear that this new Dock is designed to meet, not only the requirements of the Mercantile Marine, but also of the Royal Navy, and will be able to accommodate the largest of our modern battleships. You, Mr. Chairman, and your co-Trustees, are to be complimented on your far-seeing policy. For, profitting by past experiences, you have determined that the work which we now inaugurate shall not be calculated for present demands alone, but be sufficient to meet all possible needs and development of commerce for many years to come. The fact that the suggestion of the Board of Admiralty to increase the width of the entrance of the new Wet and Dry Docks from 90 to 100 feet was readily complied with is, indeed, a proof that a spirit of patriotism inspires the administration of the Trust.

I am glad to know that your resources are such that there is no anticipation of this enlargement of the Port facilities increasing the charges levied upon Trade.

The decision that the name of this extension to the Prince's and Victoria Docks shall be the

"Alexandra Dock" will, I am sure, be most gratifying to my dear mother.

I thank you sincerely for the cordial reception which you have given to the Princess and myself, and for the beautiful and artistic casket containing the address, which we shall greatly value as a specimen of the work of the School of Art of your City.

CENTRAL INDIA CHIEFS, INDORE.

[On November 16th, His Majesty made a brief address to the Central India Chiefs at Indore, the same being translated by Major Daly into Hindustani :—]

Will you tell the Chiefs of Central India how glad I am to have this opportunity of seeing them? As they already know, I had hoped to meet some of them at Agra where I should have exchanged visits with them. But owing to the scarcity which has befallen Rajputana our tour has been changed at the last moment, and I have been enabled to come to Indore where, by a fortunate chance, nearly all the Chiefs of Central India are assembled. I wish you to explain to them that I, like the members of my house, attach great importance to the observance of ceremonial customs, and if time had allowed I should have exchanged visits with the Chiefs as I did in Bombay. But time does not allow and I must count myself fortunate that I am able to see them at to-day's Durbar. My visit here is of a somewhat informal character and I wish you clearly to explain to all present that my omission which arises purely from a lack of time is to form no precedent, nor detract from privileges and customs which I cherish and esteem as dearly as any Chief in India.

REPLY TO UDAIPUR MAHARANA.

[On the 18th November, His Majesty visited Udaipur, the oldest Rajput State of India, and here he made one of his most graceful speeches, in reply to that of the Maharana. He said :—]

Maharana Sahib,—On behalf of the Princess of Wales and myself I thank you with all my heart for the charming manner in which you have proposed our healths. We are both delighted that our first visit as the guests of an Indian prince should have been to your beautiful capital. All India is still somewhat strange to us, but in Mewar we are truly in a new world, and from the moment when we arrived in your State this morning to this hour, one charming impression has been quickly followed by another.

We have heard much of the Rajputs, and have had the pleasure of meeting those of your class in England, but to realise the splendid traditions of chivalry, freedom, and courtesy, which are the proud possessions of the Rajput, one must see him in his own home, and for the Princess and myself, I say, in all sincerity, that all we have heard and read in the praise of Rajputana, is dwarfed by what we have seen in one short day.

It would be almost superfluous to speak to those present this evening about the noble reputation which Your Highness has won for yourself in Rajputana and in India, for they have all enjoyed the pleasure and the privilege, experienced by the Princess and myself to-day, of seeing and conversing with the famous Chief of the Sesodias. Great traditions have been greatly maintained, from what we see here in our host.

In conclusion I must convey to you the King-Emperor's message of kindness and good-will. He could not come to Udaipur. The Princess and I, as Your Highness has pointed out, are more fortunate, and thanks to the railway enterprise of the Maharana, we have been able to reach this old-world city in ease and comfort. I now ask you Ladies and Gentlemen, to drink to the long life and happiness of His Highness the Maharana of Udaipur.

REPLY TO JAIPUR ADDRESS.

[His Majesty did not visit Ajmere as originally proposed, but he made an interesting reply to the Municipal address that was presented to him. His Majesty's kindly feelings are manifest in every line of it :—]

Gentlemen,—In the name of the Princess of Wales and on my own behalf I thank you for the expression of hearty greeting and goodwill which are contained in your address. You have already received from me the message of sympathy which I sent to you from England; and if anything could add to our sincere regret it is that we should be receiving you here in Jaipur and not in your own city. It is a very charming description which you have given of Ajmer's history and attractions. We both feel strongly for you in your troubles, and after the long series of your misfortunes, we hope that a happy period of prosperity is in store for Ajmer and Rajputana.

The design on the casket will serve as an imperishable record of the beautiful architecture of Ajmer, and I am glad to read of the restoration of Shah Jehan's pavilion. I am equally interested to hear of the Mayo College; you may well be proud to have such an institution in your midst. Both of these will be for all time associated with the name and the energies of your late Viceroy, Lord Curzon.

Your historical sketch is one from which both you and I may draw satisfaction, and I shall be very glad to acquaint the King-Emperor with your loyal expressions. It will be a pleasure to him, as it is to us, to know that you regard his house as the symbol of peace, justice and prosperity.

JAIPUR BANQUET.

[His Majesty's speech at Jaipur on November 23rd was quite a sympathetic one. He said :—]

The Princess of Wales and I are sincerely touched by the feeling words in which Your Highness has proposed our healths, and we are grateful to you, Ladies and Gentlemen, for the manner in which you have responded to this toast. Happily we can claim Your Highness as an old friend, for in all the brilliant company which assembled in London to take part in the Coronation of the King-Emperor there was no more striking or respected personality than that of the Maharaja of Jaipur. His retinue on that occasion—for his Highness travelled to England with all the circumstance of a Rajput Chief and the observances of a Great Hindu—prepared us in some measure for the feudal splendours which we see around us in this exquiste capital. But we had no idea of Jaipur itself—its perfect city and the well ordered administration of the State.

We have most unfortunately arrived in Your Highness' country at a time when your people are threatened with scarcity. But the Chief who with noble munificence founded the Indian People's Famine Fund may well be trusted to see that every measure shall be taken to alleviate the wants of his own subjects, and we have listened with feelings of the deepest satisfaction to Your Highness' announcement that you and the Maharani intend to commemorate our visit to Jaipur by respectively presenting three lakhs and one lakh of rupees to the Indian People's Famine Fund. We are greatly touched by this fresh proof of Your Highness' generosity and of your sympathy with those in distress. Believe me that no building—indeed no form of memorial of our visit—could be more acceptable to us than this addition to the funds of the great national work of mercy of which you yourself were the founder.

I was much interested yesterday in seeing the Imperial Service Transport Corps which is maintained by you in so efficient a condition, primarily for the defence of India. I rejoice to think that the Corps has been able to win laurels, not only in military campaigns, but also in the strenuous war which His Highness wages against famine.

The hospitality of the Rajputs is proverbial, and we shall carry away with us the happiest recollections of our stay in Jaipur, and I shall always remember with the greatest pleasure that I shot my first tiger in your forest.

In conclusion I wish to convey to Your Highness the message entrusted to me by the King-Emperor, who desires me to express his fervent hope that you and your State may in the future enjoy all possible blessings and prosperity. I call upon you, Ladies and Gentlemen, to join with us in drinking the health of our friend the Maharaja of Jaipur and in wishing that he may long be spared to his subjects and to India.

REPLY TO BIKANIR MAHARAJAH.

[His Majesty's speech at Bikanir, delivered on 27th November, was, owing to his indisposition, read by the Hon. Mr. Colvin, Agent to the Governor-General. In it, His Majesty made a graceful reference to his old friendship with the Maharajah :—]

I thank Your Highness most sincerely for the kind words in which you have proposed the healths of the Princess of Wales and myself. It is a great pleasure and satisfaction to us that we have been able to avail ourselves of your kind invitation to visit you at Bikanir. Thanks to your friendly welcome and generous hospitality, you have made us feel as if we were at home. In any case the Maharajah's face is very familiar to us and our children, for, besides having had the pleasure of seeing him in England two years ago, there hangs at Marlborough House an excellent portrait of His Highness, his gift to me, in the uniform of the Bikanir Camel Corps.

I have been much struck by the fine soldier-like appearance of that force. We know what they have done on active service. It will give me much pleasure to tell the King-Emperor of the smart appearance of the men, most of whom wear the medals for China and Somaliland, and of the excellent condition of the camels. I shall assure His Majesty that he has every reason to be proud of Your Highness' contribution to the Imperial Service Troops, and also inform him of your further generous offer to augment it by the addition of half of your Infantry regiment.

We have always heard of your interesting city and how your great ancestors in times past won for themselves the proud and appropriate title of Lords of the Desert, but, coming here, we realise how, through your enterprise and artistic knowledge, you have, as it were, raised from the desert a palace beautiful in its architectural design and construction and replete with every comfort, which you have so hospitably placed at our disposal. The Princess and I are much gratified to learn that Your Highness proposes to commemorate our visit by erecting a building for a library, which will also contain the beautiful and historic armoury of Bikanir. We heartily approve of Your Highness' suggestion and I am proud to think that it is your wish to call it after me.

You have also permitted me to see and enjoy what may fairly be described as one of the wonders of Bikanir—its sport. My experience of two delightful mornings' shooting at Gujner will never be forgotten.

In conclusion, I w'sh to deliver the message of friendship and good wishes to yourself and your State from the King-Emperor, to whom I shall gladly communicate your assurances of loyalty and devotion to his Throne and Person, and I ask all present to join in drinking long health and happiness to the Maharaja of Bikanir. I did not say good-bye to him this evening, for I am glad to think that he will join my staff as my Aide-de-Camp at the coming manœuvres in the north, and if anything could further add to my debt of gratitude for all His Highness' hospitality, it is the ready and considerate manner in which he has excused my attendance at this banquet in accordance with the recommendations of my medical adviser, which decision I deeply regret.

REPLY TO RAJPUTANA CHIEFS.

[Eleven Rajputana Chiefs were forced by the imminent prospect of famine to forego the pleasure of receiving and honouring His Majesty. They gave open expression to their regret in a letter of the Hon'ble Mr. Colvin to Sir Walter Lawrence, dated 26th November, 1905. To this letter, His Majesty made the following reply on the 27th November:—]

Dear Mr. Colvin,—Sir Walter Lawrence has made known to me the contents of your letter of the 26th instant, and has handed me the *kharitas* and other communications which you have received from the eleven Chiefs of Rajputana, with whom, unfortunately, owing to the circumstances recounted in your letter, I have been unable to exchange visits.

Pray assure them how greatly the Princess and I regret that we could not carry out our original wish to see them at Ajmer, and, failing that, at Agra. Tell them how heartily we reciprocate the feeling in their message. At the same time I will ask you to send them the portraits of myself which I had hoped to hand to them personally. We were equally sorry that our visit to Bhartpur had to be abandoned.

Will you also take the earliest opportunity of expressing to the Tazimi Istimrardars of Ajmer, how disappointed I am to have been unable to make their acquaintance? I am glad that we shall have the pleasure of seeing the Chiefs of Dholpur and Kishangarh at Calcutta.

Believe me,

Sincerely yours,

GEORGE P.

REPLY TO LAHORE MUNICIPALITY.

[On 28th November, His Majesty made a sympathetic reply to the Lahore Municipal address. He remarked :—]

Gentlemen,—The Princess and myself thank you most sincerely for the frank and generous welcome that you have given us in this famous capital of the Punjab. Your allusion to the calamities which have befallen you is typical of a country of brave, strong men, and grieved as the Princess and I are that the Punjab should be afflicted by earthquakes and scarcity, it is some consolation to think that these disasters do tend to bring the people and the official classes closer together.

It interests me everywhere to realise the great changes which have taken place since my dear father visited India. Perhaps in no part of the Empire are these changes more marked than in the Punjab. Railways have greatly altered the conditions of your Province, but you have justly selected irrigation as the most noteworthy of the agencies of change. Until quite recently we had no idea of the boldness and magnitude of the great schemes which are rapidly adding new districts to the Punjab. All honour to the Engineers of the Irrigation Department who have devised these splendid works! But we may be thankful, too, that in this fine country the people are ready to move their homes to the new lands.

I am glad that your town shares in the general prosperity of the Province. I trust it will continue and increase. We shall, in a short time, have an opportunity of seeing the men who have won for the Punjab the name of The Sword Hand of India. Lahore has reason to be proud of being the capital of such a nursery of devoted and loyal soldiers. We are both of us profoundly conscious of the importance of the concluding sentence of your address. The King-Emperor, to whom it will be my pleasing duty to communicate your loyal assurances, will rejoice to receive your testimony that the people are happy and contented, and will be touched by your eloquent expressions of love and attachment to His Majesty and to the late Queen-Empress.

REPLY TO PESHWAR ADDRESS.

[On December 3, His Majesty visited Peshawar, the frontier city of India, and in replying to the address presented to him on behalf of the N.-W. Frontier Province, said :—]

Gentlemen,—I thank you on behalf of the Princess of Wales and myself for the sincere, frank words with which you welcome us to the North-West Frontier Province. I shall communicate your loyal and grateful assurances to my dear father the King-Emperor. It was one of the regrets of his Indian visit that he was unable to see Peshwar, but thirty years ago there was no railway to your interesting and important city. There have been many other changes in the country across the Indus since my father visited India, and I am rejoiced to learn that those changes have tended towards your happiness and prosperity. Security and order are blessings for which we may all be thankful, and I have little fear that in this free, hardy country "tranquillity and rest" will impair the many qualities of the Pathan. The Princess and I fervently pray that the peace which you now enjoy may long continue. You are the wardens of the Passes, and from far across the seas the British people watch you with sympathy and confidence.

REPLY TO JAMMU MAHARAJAH.

[Responding, on 10th December, to the sonorous Address of the Maharajah of Jammu and Kashmir, His Majesty spoke in the following terms :—]

Maharaja Sahib,—I thank you most warmly for the charming manner in which you have proposed the healths of the Princess of Wales and myself. We are both of us delighted to be the guests of this famous State of Jammu and Kashmir. Thirty years ago my dear father enjoyed the hospitality of Maharaja Runbir Singh and he has never forgotten the splendid and loyal welcome which he received at the hands of the Chief of the Dogras.

In England we are perhaps more familiar with the beauty and fair fame of the Vale of Kashmir than we are with the less known, but not less honourable, record of Jammu. I wish that circumstances could have enabled us to accept the Maharaja's oft-repeated invitation to visit Kashmir, but His Highness knows how difficult it has been to do all that we wished to accomplish. We should, however, have been truly disappointed if we had been obliged to forego the pleasure of a visit to Jammu, for I wished to have an opportunity of doing honour to a Chief who has in a marked degree thrown in his lot with the fortunes of the Indian Empire. I wish on this occasion to record the appreciation which is felt by me and my fellow-countrymen of the brave and important services which His Highness and his Imperial Service Troops have rendered to our Empire on the distant frontiers of his State.

I am rejoiced to hear of the great public works which His Highness is so wisely undertaking. They will undoubtedly add to the prosperity of his State and his subjects, and are of a magnitude sufficient to make Kashmir famous even in this progressive age. I am glad, too, that the Maharaja is making efforts to give the advantages of higher education to his people and am delighted to think that our stay here is to be associated with a college to be called after me.

Our visit to Jammu happily coincides with a constitutional change in the Government of Jammu and Kashmir. Ladies and Gentlemen, in asking you to join the Princess and myself in drinking the health of His Highness the Maharaja, I feel sure that we shall all most fervently wish that the change to which I have alluded will bring to him honour and peace of mind, and to his people security and happiness.

To Face Page 32.

THEIR MAJESTIES WITH THEIR CHILDREN.

REPLY TO AMRITSAR MUNICIPAL COUNCIL.

[On 11th December, His Majesty spoke as follows in replying to the address of welcome presented by the Amritsar Municipality :—]

Gentlemen—I thank you on behalf of the Princess of Wales and myself for the kind words in which you welcome us to this celebrated city. We were both most anxious to see as much as possible of the famous centres of India, and we could not leave the Punjab without alighting at the place which is so dear to those good soldiers—the Sikhs. If time had allowed we should gladly have prolonged our stay in Amritsar, but even our short visit here will add to those lasting impressions which we shall carry away with us. Here as elsewhere, there has been great progress since my dear father visited you thirty years ago, and we rejoice to hear of the increase in your wealth, trade, education, and sanitation. It would seem to be most appropriate that the Khalsa College should have been instituted in this city, so sacred to the men of the Khalsa race. Renowned as is

Amritsar for its commerce, it may be that some day it will be equally renowned as the great centre of Sikh education. It will please the King-Emperor, to whom I shall gladly tender your loyal expressions, to receive your acknowledgment of the peace and prosperity which you enjoy under his rule. We both of us hope that these blessings may long attend you and your city.

AT KHALSA COLLEGE.

[Speaking later at the Khalsa College, His Majesty said :—]

The Princess of Wales joins with me in sincerely thanking the Khalsa College Council, and the Managing Committee, for the kind sentiments to which their address gives expression. We are glad to have the opportunity to-day of visiting this College, which may indeed claim to be representative of the Sikhs, supported as it is by all classes of that community. I appreciate highly the manly qualities of the Sikhs, and their loyalty and devotion. It affords me sincere pleasure to find that they have realized the importance of education in the present age, and have taken steps to promote its spread among themselves. The future success of the movement depends on their steadfastly maintaining the effort they have initiated. With the continuing interest of the venerable Rajah of Nabha, who has done so much for the Institution, and with all ranks co-operating, success should be ensured, and I earnestly trust that the hopes expressed in your address for the completion of the buildings may speedily be fulfilled.

REPLY TO DELHI MUNICIPALITY.

[His Majesty arrived at Delhi, the imperial city, on December 12th, now nearly six years ago. The Municipality read an address of welcome, and, in his reply, His Majesty touched on the inherent vitality of the great city. He said :—]

Gentlemen,—Both the Princess of Wales and I have been looking forward with much pleasure to seeing your historic city, and we thank you heartily for the reception which you have given us and for the kind words of welcome which you have used in your address. The beautiful city which is in your keeping has been the scene of many stirring incidents and splendid pageants. She seems to have the power, inherent in some great capitals, of attracting and compelling attention, and to the Princess and myself this visit will be rich in reflections on the past and in thoughts of the future.

That the proud position of Delhi is still unshaken is proved by the very material and important fact of the many railways which now run to her walls. They do not come to your city for any other reasons than those of trade, and it seems to me that you are as fortunate in your great commercial future as you have been in your distinguished political past.

I shall gladly inform the King-Emperor of your gratitude for the advantages of peace, civilization and railway enterprise, and I have no doubt that you will make the best of these undoubted advantages. It is in the power of you and your successors to maintain that position which Delhi has always held in this great Indian Empire.

AT AGRA.

[On the 17th December following, His Majesty reached Agra, the earlier Moghul capital of India. In responding to the Municipal Welcome Address, he remarked :—]

Gentlemen,—On behalf of the Princess of Wales and myself I thank you sincerely for the kind welcome which you have given to us. It is a privilege to any one, whether from the West or from the East, to approach your beautiful and historical city. We look forward with keen interest to seeing its artistic and architectural beauties of which you are so justly proud ; and I am quite certain that, during our visit, we shall gain impressions of Agra which will never fade from our minds, and we shall always remember your friendly greeting and the pains which you have taken to make our stay here pleasant and successful.

I look forward to associating myself with you in the unveiling, on Monday, of the statue which you have raised to the memory of our late beloved Queen-Empress. It is befitting that in this city, so rich in exquisite monuments of the great Emperor of the past, there should be a memorial of a ruler who yielded to none in her love and goodwill towards India. Nothing can rob you of the noble inheritance which you possess.

I notice with satisfaction that you are keeping pace with the times, so that you have a future, as well as a past, for I learn that your railway system is being further developed, and that your cotton industry is steadily increasing. Gentlemen, the Princess and I earnestly trust that the prosperity and welfare of Agra may thus continue. I shall have much pleasure in conveying to the King-Emperor those assurances of your undying devotion to His Majesty to which your address gives expression.

UNVEILING VICTORIA STATUE.

[Unveiling the statue of the late Queen Victoria, Agra, His Majesty said :—]

Gentlemen,—When some months ago I accepted your invitation to unveil this statue of our late beloved Queen-Empress, my intention was to perform the ceremony in silence, for on occasions like this, when our hearts are full of hallowed memories, silence is often more eloquent than the sincerest words of praise and affection. But, Gentlemen, your address has greatly touched the Princess of Wales and myself, and we wish to join in this tribute of love and gratitude to her whom you simply, but truly, call, a "Great and Noble Queen." No words of mine are needed to tell you that my revered grandmother loved the Indian people, and that she bequeathed to my dear father, and to me, her great regard for India. I unveil this statue, not only as a memorial of your first Queen-Empress, but also as a memorial to the fact that India knows how to be grateful for her love. It will be an enduring monument of the sympathy which existed between the Queen-Empress Victoria and her Indian people. May such feelings of attachment to our House grow stronger and stronger as time goes on!

AT GWALIOR.

[Gwalior was reached on 20th December, and before opening the New Market and the Electrical Installation, at Lashkar, His Majesty said :—]

Your Highness and Members of the Municipal Committee of Lashkar,—It has given the Princess of Wales and myself great satisfaction to accept your interesting address, and to observe from it that in matters of local self-government the Gwalior State is adopting a wise and forward policy. I have much pleasure in acceding to your request that I should open the Victoria Memorial Market, and inaugurate the City's installation of electric lighting. I trust that for many years to come these undertakings will prove of benefit to the City of Lashkar, and bear testimony to the enterprise of its Municipality and the philanthropic zeal of His Highness the Maharaja.

REPLY TO GWALIOR MAHARAJAH.

[In replying to the Maharajah Scindiah of Gwalior, on 20th December, he said :—]

Maharaja Sahib,—In the name of the Princess of Wales and on my own behalf, I thank you sincerely for the eloquent and touching words in which you have proposed our healths. I recognise that we have listened to no mere complimentary speech, but that His Highness has taken this opportunity of telling us the guiding principles and motives of his life. We are, I am sure, grateful for his frankness, and highly appreciate his noble expressions; for whether we regard these principles from the point of view of the British Empire the Maharaja himself, or the subjects of the Gwalior State, we cannot fail to recognise in them the highest ideals and aspirations. His goal is the stability of the British Empire, and to attain that goal, he sees that he must strive, and indeed he is striving with all his characteristic energy, to improve the condition of his people. I look forward with pleasure and interest to hearing from His Highness of his administrative reforms.

And while His Highness modestly refrained from telling us of his ambitions and intentions, we do not forget the hospital ship which he sent to China a few years ago. I should like also to remind you of the two regiments which the Maharaja has just added to the Imperial Service Troops; and, indeed, I believe that his ambition is to see his whole army attain to that excellence which characterises the troops which he gives so freely to the service of the Empire; and I should like to say how very much I am indebted to him for showing me his fine troops on parade this morning.

We all know of our host's reputation as a soldier, but his energies and his influence are just as conspicuous and effective in the Civil administration of his State. The Princess and I desire to express our deep sense of gratitude to Your Highness for the kindness and hospitality which you have shown to us and for all the trouble which you have taken to entertain us and our large party in your capital; nor can I refrain from alluding to the magnificent procession with which Your Highness honoured our arrival yesterday. It was the first time that we had taken part in a ceremony mounted on elephants, which is only possible in this wonderful country. I can assure you that we shall never forget that splendid scene with all its picturesque surroundings, and we shall also remember that every one of its details had been conceived and carried out so successfully by Your Highness. I am looking forward with great pleasure to enjoying the sport for which your State is so well renowned, and in which you are kind enough to allow me to join.

Before sitting down, I must convey to you, Maharaja, my dear father's warm messages of esteem and goodwill, and I am glad to have another message to deliver from the King-Emperor which I am sure will please Your Highness. You have been appointed Honorary Colonel of the Indian Regiment, of which I am proud to be the Colonel-in-Chief; the 1st Lancers will be as delighted as I am to welcome you as one of us. I call upon you, Ladies and Gentlemen, to join with me in drinking to the health and long life of His Highness the Maharaja Scindia, and pray that all possible blessings may be given to him and to his people.

REPLY TO LUCKNOW MUNICIPALITY.

[At Lucknow, on the 26th December, His Majesty, thus addressed the local Municipality :—]

Gentlemen,—The Princess of Wales and I are very grateful to you for the kind words of your address. It is, indeed, a great undertaking to travel through this vast Indian Empire. Time would not permit of our visiting all of the many places we wished to see, but we made a point of including in our programme a visit to your famous and interesting City. The name of Lucknow is very precious to us at Home. It is part of our history of which we are proud, and these sentiments of pride may be shared by the gallant Veterans whom I hope to see this afternoon at the Residency. None of us can forget the significant fact commemorated by the monument erected by Lord Northbrook to the brave Indians who fought by our side. I am told, and I believe it, that the same feelings which inspired them animate the people of Oudh to-day. We both hope to enjoy our stay in Lucknow, to study its historical landmarks, and to meet the great Talukdars of Oudh. I shall not fail to convey to the King-Emperor your loyal assurances. We thank you for your friendly welcome, and we wish you all the prosperity which should attend the capital of the Garden of India.

LUCKNOW MEDICAL COLLEGE,

LAYING FOUNDATION STONE.

[Laying the foundation-stone of the new Medical College, at Lucknow, His Royal Highness said :—]

Sir John Stanley and Gentlemen,—On behalf of the Princess of Wales and myself, I thank you sincerely for the very kind sentiments to which your address gives expression; we also thank you for affording us this opportunity of identifying ourselves with an institution which must have a marked influence on the health and happiness of the vast population of these provinces. I gather from papers which I have read, that for many years the need of a Medical College has been recognised. I rejoice to think that, thanks to the noble liberality of the Maharaja of Bulrampur and of others whose names will be gratefully remembered by future generations, this great need will now be supplied. We deem ourselves fortunate that the year of our visit should have seen the fulfilment of this great idea, for I have inherited from my dear parents their keen interest and deep sympathy in all that concerns the noble art and profession of healing. I believe there are many special points connected with this Medical College on which I may congratulate you and your Lieutenant-Governor, Sir James La Touche. The movement is the spontaneous outcome of the peoples' wishes, and so a movement which is healthy and will endure; and it is a movement in which all classes, high and low, rich and poor, official and non-official, have taken a part. I must congratulate you also on the splendid site which you have secured; high and healthy, but still in the close neighbourhood of your City. And lastly, I am desired by the Princess to congratulate you on the special provision which, thanks to the initiative and generosity of Raja Tassaday Rasul Khan, has been made for the education of women. If the Medical College becomes, as I hope it will, "the best in the East," a very powerful stimulus will be given to the movement which will always be associated with the name of Lady Dufferin. I am delighted to lay the foundation-stone of the College and we are proud that our names will be respectively associated with the Institution and its branch College for Women.

TALUKDARS' ADDRESS.

[Replying to the address of the Talukdars of Oudh, His Majesty spoke as follows :—]

The Princess of Wales and myself are very glad to meet you, the Talukdars of Oudh, in this great hall, where just thirty years ago my dear father, our King-Emperor, first made your acquaintance. I thank you for the splendid reception which you have given to us in this historic capital of Oudh, and I rejoice to hear that your connection with the British Crown has brought you prosperity and happiness. It is pleasant to hear that you can say in all sincerity that your rights and privileges have been recognised and respected by the British Government. The best guarantee of your valued privileges lies in your allegiance and loyalty to the King-Emperor, and your warm assurances shall be communicated to him without delay.

The Princess and I are delighted to hear of the steady progress of Oudh in moral and material paths. The pleasant and hopeful account which you gave in your address is due to the fact that, though adhering to your status and privileges, you still wisely move with the times. I hope that you and your descendants will follow this wise policy, and that whenever other members of our House may, like us, be fortunate enough to visit India, they will find the Talukdars of Oudh as contented and as kind and courteous as those whom I have the pleasure of addressing this evening. I heartily thank you all for the beautiful entertainment which you have given in our honour. We shall never forget the Talukdars of Oudh and their generous hospitality.

REPLY TO CALCUTTA CORPORATION.

[At Calcutta, the City of Palaces, His Majesty was welcomed by the Corporation and in responding to its address, he said :—]

The magnificent spectacle which you have afforded to the Princess of Wales and myself, the vast crowds which are assembled to welcome us, and the eloquent words of your address, will remain among our most memorable experiences of this great Empire and its peoples. We both know that we are merely the fortunate recipients of the loyalty which the citizens of Calcutta feel for the King-Emperor, and in conveying to him your utterances of allegiance and devotion, I shall endeavour to describe the impressive scene on which we are now looking.

There is, perhaps, nothing in the whole of India more typical of the relations between the British and Indians than Calcutta, which has grown from a river swamp to be the second city of our Empire. If, as you say, the prosperity that blesses this place is common to all India, we may congratulate ourselves on the results of the bond between the Mother Country and India. Every citizen of this great capital may feel a legitimate pride in the wonderful town that has sprung up on the Hughli, and our fellow subjects in other parts of the Empire will see in Calcutta present prosperity and future growth—the sign which I recognise everywhere of a union which, under God's providence, seems destined to endure. It is a great pleasure to the Princess and to myself that she has been able to accompany me to India, and on her behalf I thank you most heartily for the beautiful gift which Calcutta so generously offers her, and which she will always treasure as a charming remembrance of our visit and a token of affection and good-will.

ALL-INDIA VICTORIA MEMORIAL LAYING FOUNDATION STONE.

[In laying the foundation stone, at the same city, of the All-India Victoria Memorial, he remarked:—]

Sir Andrew Fraser and Gentlemen,—We are met to-day to commemorate a great sorrow and a great love. Everywhere the Princess of Wales and myself, in our journey through this vast and varied land, have had almost daily evidence of the ample manner in which India has returned the affection of her first Queen-Empress. This sentiment, so touching and so precious, finds its highest and most universal expression in the National Monument with which the Princess and I are proud to be associated to-day. We have heard from Sir Andrew Fraser of the difficulties which attended the initial stages of this great memorial, and we must all of us recognise that it is to Lord Curzon's untiring energy and devotion that the tribute to the late Queen-Empress has taken this national and far-reaching aspect. I am glad to know that the interest which he took in the building of this hall will not cease with his departure from India, but he will continue to show his sympathy with the undertaking. It is right and befitting that there should be memorials in all parts of India in honour of one who, though never privileged to see her Indian subjects in their own countries, seemed to have the peculiar power of being in touch and in sympathy with all classes of this continent. But it is still more befitting that there should be one memorial in India—a symbol of the unity and concord which came from her all-embracing love for her people and an enduring token of the affection which all—Europeans and Indians, Princes and peasants—felt for Queen Victoria.

To us this wonderful expression of gratitude brings natural pride and warm hopes. The Taj, which has delighted and fascinated us by its beauty and by its story, can never be rivalled in its grace. But in generations to come this memorial to a great Queen, whose sympathy conquered distance and space, may present to the historian reflections as hallowed as those which are inspired by the Taj Mahal. I congratulate the Executive Committee and the Trustees of this great All-Indian Trust on the success which has attended their patient labour of love. It will gain from Lord Minto further strength and encouragement, and I feel sure that the same spirit of affection and veneration which has brought this splendid and most worthy memorial into being will, under His Excellency's guiding influence, cherish and quicken its future progress. I must thank you, Sir Andrew Fraser, for your concluding words, which will be as gratifying to my dear father as they are inspirating to the Princess and myself. I will now, with much pleasure and with feelings of profound gratitude to all who have shared in this most noble endeavour, proceed to lay the foundation-stone of the Victoria Memorial Hall. Among the many interesting ceremonies in which we have taken part during our stay in India, I can assure you that none could have appealed more to our hearts than the opening act of this great work.

REPLY TO RANGOON MUNICIPALITY.

[In reply to the Rangoon Municipal address, His Majesty spoke as follows :—]

The Princess of Wales and myself are most grateful to you for the hearty welcome you have given to us in your great and growing city. In your address you have struck the note which must predominate over all others in the minds of those who visit India and Burma for the first time. It is a source of never-ending wonder and satisfaction to me to notice the extraordinary variety of races, religions and languages which are so harmoniously blended in the large centres of the Indian Empire. This harmony is due to the wise policy of tolerance for all creeds, and of equal justice for all races, and is the basis and the secret of the marvellous administration of which we in England are so proud, and for which you and all those who are working for this country, whether as officials or non-officials, British or Orientals, are entitled to all praise.

We only wish that it could have been arranged that our stay in this bright and vigorous province could be longer, but, as you know, we have a long journey before us and dates are hard masters. Still the Princess and I trust that, even in the short time we shall spend in your country, we shall gain some knowledge and much sympathy for Burma, which will enable us in the years to come to watch its progress and development with interest and the most confident hope. The heartiness of your welcome, your beautiful decorations—which point to kindly labour and infinite pains—and cheery faces which greet us on our arrival, all go to confirm us in our previous ideas of Burma and its peoples. May you long retain your reputation for genial content and happy life.

OPENING RANGOON VICTORIA MEMORIAL PARK.

[Opening the Victoria Memorial Park at Rangoon, His Majesty said :—]

The Princess of Wales and I desire to thank the people of Rangoon, and of Burma generally, for the kind words with which they have, through you, welcomed us here to-day. It is a great pleasure to us to join with them in the inauguration of this Park which is your memorial to our late beloved Queen. I congratulate you on the fitness of dedicating to her memory a place where the highest and lowest alike can breathe the fresh air and rejoice the eye in the beauties of Nature, for Queen Victoria set great store by these gifts, and she always sought for rest from the fatigues of her busy, active life in the fresh air amidst all those country scenes and surroundings which she loved so well. And no less would she have rejoiced to think that, in clearing the land for this place of public recreation, insanitary buildings had been swept away and the occupants given sites in new and healthy areas.

I note with satisfaction that the principal donors comprise representatives of all the varied races which constitute the population of Rangoon, and it is gratifying to know that those of our fellow subjects in India "who have made for themselves homes in Burma" are ready to contribute from their wealth acquired in this country towards the beautifying of its capital. On the other hand I am glad to learn, from the Chairman's speech, that the scheme was favoured and supported by a very large number of persons of more moderate means who have also contributed to the Fund. I now have much pleasure in declaring the Victoria Memorial Park open, and the Princess and I earnestly trust that it may prove a joy and blessing to the people of Burma for all time.

REPLY TO MANDALAY MUNICIPALITY.

[In acknowledging the address of the Mandalay Municipality, His Majesty said :—]

It is a great pleasure to the Princess of Wales and myself to visit Mandalay and to see the picturesque and interesting head-quarters of Upper Burma. I thank you heartily for the cordial welcome which you have given to us, and I am confident that your kind efforts to make our stay in Mandalay agreeable will be crowned with success. I wish that we could have stayed longer with you for, in some ways, Upper Burma possesses a peculiar interest in that it is the latest addition to the British Empire. If I may judge from what I have heard, and from what I now see, Upper Burma has very rapidly advanced to the level and standard of British India, and I can certainly detect no signs of backwardness or stagnation. I will, with pleasure, convey your loyal assurances to the King-Emperor; he will be especially interested to hear of your welfare and will be touched when I tell him of the devotion to his person which is manifested in the enthusiastic reception which you have given to the Princess and myself.

MADRAS.

[His Majesty arrived at Madras, on board the *Hyacinth*, on 24th January, 1906. Responding to the Madras Corporation's address, he said :—]

Gentlemen,—I thank you for the hearty welcome which you offer to the Princess of Wales and myself. We have looked forward with much pleasure to visiting your old and historic city, which I believe to be our oldest possession and the oldest municipality in British India, and I desire to express our deep appreciation of the generous efforts and carefully planned preparations which have been made for our reception by you and the citizens of Madras. We anticipate with interest the scenes which await us during the next few days and we hope to use the opportunities which you and my friend, Lord Ampthill, have given us for seeing your City and its people. I will not fail to communicate to the King-Emperor your loyal assurances. Though thirty years have passed since he was your guest, my dear father's recollections of Madras are still vivid and happy. Gentlemen, I again thank you for the affectionate terms in which you have greeted us to your city.

REPLY TO MADRAS LAND HOLDERS' ADDRESS.

[Replying to the address of the Madras Land-holders' Association, His Majesty said :—]

Gentlemen,—It is a great pleasure to the Princess of Wales and myself to have this opportunity of meeting the members of your important Association and I heartily thank you for the welcome which you offer to us. We have noticed with satisfaction your genuine feelings of devotion to the person of the Sovereign. Everywhere we have had proofs of the same loyal sentiment, but nowhere has it been more eloquently expressed than here in Southern India. I shall be very glad to communicate your assurances to the King-Emperor and to tell him that our visit to Madras has been the occasion for this enthusiastic demonstration. With you I earnestly hope that our visit to India will not be without useful results. Already the Princess and I begin to feel that we are at home and that we understand much that no books and no amount of study would have revealed to us. We both recognise the serious importance of our mission to India and we pray that it may be fruitful both to you and to us. We thank you most heartily for all that you have said and we both of us wish all prosperity to the Members of your Association.

OPENING VICTORIA TECHNICAL INSTITUTE.

[Speaking at the opening of the Victoria Technical Institute, he said :—]

It is a great pleasure to the Princess of Wales and myself to take part in this ceremony—an outward and visible sign of the devotion of the people of Madras to our late lamented Queen-Empress Victoria. We are greatly touched by the feeling tones in which you speak of her beloved and venerated memory. The object of the Victoria Memorial Technical Institute, namely, to develop the talents and improve the condition of the artists and craftsmen of the Presidency, is one which, I am confident, would have appealed in every way to Queen Victoria, who always followed with interest every practical efforts which aimed at making the lives of her Indian peoples more prosperous and contended. You may rest assured that this undertaking will have the approval of my dear father, the King-Emperor, as it has the sympathy of the Princess of Wales and myself. It is interesting to know that a movement set on foot to commemorate the Queen-Empress' Jubilee in 1897 has seen its consummation in a memorial to her long and glorious reign.

I am gratified to learn your address of the generous assistance and co-operation which the movement has received from your Governor, Lord Ampthill, and that you are indebted to the Government of Madras for the site and for a considerable grant towards the Building Fund. I congratulate you upon the valuable honorary services which have been rendered in the Administrative Council of the Institute since its formation in 1887. The Princess of Wales and I sincerely trust that the Victoria Memorial Technical Institute may, in every way, fulfil the high ideal of its Founders and conduce to the further prosperity and general well-being of the people of this Presidency.

REPLY TO CITIZENS' ADDRESS.

[Replying to the address of the citizens of Madras, His Majesty remarked :—]

Gentlemen,—I was very glad to hear from your Governor, Lord Ampthill, that I should have an opportunity of meeting you, the representatives of the great Presidency of Madras and of the States of Travancore, Cochin and Pudukota. On behalf of the Princess of Wales and myself, I tender you our sincere thanks for the warm-hearted address which has just been read. We both of us do feel a "deep concern" and "lively interest" in all that affects the welfare of our fellow subjects. We fully realise the privilege which we are now enjoying of seeing these distant parts of the Empire and are most grateful for the affectionate manner in which Southern India has greeted us.

It is a great regret to both of us that we were unable to visit others of your famous cities or to stay in some of the States. We have read of Trichinopoly, Tanjore and Madura, and of the charms of Travancore and Cochin. But time will not admit of our stay in India being prolonged and it is for this reason that we are so glad to have had the chance of seeing you this evening. We shall be most grateful if you will tell your friends, when you return home, that your address in no way exaggerate, the interest and love which we have for this great country and its people.

OPENING CHAMARAJENDRA INSTITUTE, MYSORE.

[At Mysore, His Majesty laid the foundation stone of the Chamarajendra Technical Institute, and in doing so, he said :—]

Your Highness,—I am very glad to be associated with this Industrial Institution and to have an opportunity of showing my sympathy with the artisans of Mysore and of India. The Princess of Wales and I have greatly admired their work at various places on our journey and I am heartily in favour of any movement that may either tend to improve the handicrafts of India or raise the social position of the artisan. We have seen much of the arts in India but have seen very little of the artisans and I am especially delighted to take part in any ceremony which may lead towards the amelioration of one of the most deserving and most important classes of the Indian people.

MYSORE BANQUET.

[In his long reply at the of Mysore Maharajah's Banquet, His Majesty reached the high-water mark of statesmanship. He said :—]

It was a great regret to my dear father that he could not visit your State in 1875, and we consider ourselves fortunate in being able to avail ourselves of your most kind invitation to Mysore. We are delighted thus to become personally acquainted with Your Highness, to have an opportunity of gaining some experience of your State in these early days of your administration, and to visit the scenes of those stirring incidents which will live for ever in the history of Mysore, and indeed of India. It is superfluous for me to dilate on the attitude of the King-Emperor and of the late Queen-Empress towards the great ruling Chiefs of the Indian Empire. But I may take this opportunity of saying that all I have seen during my visit to India has confirmed me in my high opinion and warm appreciation of those who, like Your Highness, so steadily and loyally support the government of the King-Emperor.

If any proof were required of the wisdom of the policy of 1881, which restored to your father the province of Mysore after fifty years of British administration, it is surely to be found in the contentment and prosperity which the people of Mysore enjoy under the government of Your Highness. It is interesting to hear of the many enterprises, notably that of the Cauvery Electrical Works, and the general policy of irrigation and public works. Under the lead which we may expect from such a capable and enlightened Ruler as our kind host, with the assistance of statesmen of the type of the late Sir Seshadri Iyer, your Province may look forward with confidence to making still greater strides.

It was most gratifying to listen to Your Highness' allusion to the Imperial Service Troops, and to hear from you that among those who formed our escort yesterday and to-day are men whose ancestors fought so gallantly at Seringapatam and in the Deccan. I am told that the old fighting spirit of the South still pervades Mysore, and my own brief observations have given me some idea of the efficiency of your cavalry. I learn that your transport is equally well organised and efficient and I truly congratulate Your Highness on the valuable troops which Mysore contributes towards the defence of the Indian Empire.

I regret that your State has also suffered in common with other parts of India from the terrible visitation of the plague, but I am thankful to hear of a decided decline in the severity of the affliction, and I trust that by the mercy of God, Mysore may soon be restored to a state of happiness and prosperity.

REPLY TO BANGALORE MUNICIPALITY.

[Replying to the address of welcome presented by the Station Municipality of Bangalore, His Majesty said :—]

I thank you, on behalf of the Princess of Wales and myself, for your kind and hearty welcome to Bangalore. It is a great pleasure to us that we have been able to pay a visit to your station, for apart from its beauty and advantages of climate, Bangalore has played an important part in the history of British India. You allude to the fact that the King-Emperor was prevented from coming to Bangalore. Thirty years have brought great changes in India, and everywhere I am reminded of the enormous influence which has been exercised by the steady and strenuous railway policy of the Government of India. What was impossible at the time of my dear father's visit to India is easy, and comparativelyspeaking, comfortable to us. We have heard of the troubles which have befallen Bangalore, but trust that better days are in store for you, and that the great blessing of health may be again enjoyed by all. We shall carry away with us the pleasantest memories of your picturesque and well ordered station, and we wish you all prosperity.

UNVEILING BANGALORE VICTORIA MEMORIAL.

[Unveiling the Victoria Memorial Statue at Bangalore, His Majesty spoke in these terms :—]

I accept with the greatest pleasure your invitation to unveil this statue of our late Queen-Empress. The words which you have used make it almost superfluous for me, her grandson, to utter one word more of loving admiration. The Princess of Wales and myself have now travelled through a considerable portion of India, and nothing has given us greater pride and touched our hearts more than the universal love and veneration which is shown for the memory of her whom you aptly call "The noble Empress Victoria the Good." There is one thing about the statue which gives me especial pleasure. It is the association of the Maharaja of Mysore and his people with the inhabitants of the Civil and Military station of Bangalore. Nothing could be more in harmony with the wishes and sentiments of her to whom you have raised this statue than this comradeship and fellow-feeling.

BANGALORE.

[His Majesty, presented a new Standard to the Carabiniers at Bangalore. Committing the Standard to the regiment, he said:—]

Colonel Leader, Officers, Non-Commissioned Officers and men of the Carabiniers,—It is the first time that I have presented a Standard to a Cavalry regiment and I am especially glad to do so to a regiment which has a history so distinguished as yours. It has served ten Sovereigns. Founded in 1685, its services were rewarded only eight years later by King William III, who granted it the title of "Carabiniers," by which name the regiment has ever since been known. It gained renown upon the battlefields of the great Duke of Marlborough, while in the past century it earned fresh laurels in the campaigns of the Crimea, Indian Mutiny and South Africa. On such an occasion as this, it is only right that a regiment should recall with pride the deeds done by it in the past. I entrust this consecrated Standard to your care and I know that you will look up to it with those same feelings of loyalty to your King and country as have ever characterised the Carabiniers.

HYDERABAD STATE BANQUET.

[His Majesty was to have spoken at Hyderabad, but a sad bereavement in the household of the late Nizam prevented the holding of the State Banquet. But his speech was to have been to the following effect :—]

Your Highness,—I thank you sincerely for the generous words which you have addressed to the Princess of Wales and myself in your eloquent speech. We are deeply grateful to you for the magnificence of your reception, for your kind hospitality, for your many acts of courteous welcome, and for your friendly consideration, for our comfort. I will, without delay, inform my dear Father of your loyal assurances, and I hope to the able to describe to the King-Emperor, in some measure, the splendours of Hyderabad and the devotion of Your Highness and your people to the British Crown. It is especially gratifying to us that our visit should be the occasion of the founding of the Zenana Hospital, being both of us deeply interested in hospitals and their splendid work. On behalf of the Princess, I thank Your Highness for your touching allusions to the name of the late beloved Queen-Empress and to her own connection with that institution.

I am much gratified by your stirring words regarding the Imperial Service Troops which form part of Your Highness' Army and I know they will be highly appreciated by His Majesty. No one can speak with greater authority on this subject than our kind host, for we all know that it was the Nizam who was the first of the Princes of India to come forward with a spontaneous offer of assistance for the common cause of Imperial Defence. I have had opportunities of seeing your two fine regiments of Imperial Service Lancers and I congratulate Your Highness on their soldierly and workmanlike appearance. As this is possibly the last occasion on which we shall be the guests of an Indian Prince, I thank you most gratefully for the assurances which you have made, not only for the important State over which you rule, but for the Princes and people of India. Nothing will please His Majesty more than the concluding words of your speech, and they will be especially valued as coming from one who is pre-eminently qualified by position, experience and tradition to speak on the sentiments of the Princes and the people of India towards the British

Throne. We shall always retain the warmest feelings of regard for Your Highness and the most pleasant recollections of our visit to Hyderabad. Before I sit down I will ask you, Ladies and Gentlemen, to join me in drinking to the health of our friend and faithful ally, His Highness the Nizam.

REPLY TO BENARES MUNICIPAL BOARD.

[Replying to the Benares Municipal Board, on 19th February, 1906, His Majesty said :—]

Gentlemen,—The Princess of Wales and myself have been deeply touched by the affectionate greeting accorded to us in the great centres of India, and nowhere more than at this historic city, so dear and so sacred to the millions of the Hindu people; and I feel that I cannot do better than recall the words of my dear father, spoken thirty years ago, when he expressed the intense pleasure which he felt in being received in the centre of all the nations and people of Hindu origin. And as our time in India is rapidly drawing to an end, we feel an especial satisfaction that a visit to this important and interesting home of Hinduism should be one of the last of our impressions on the delightful tour which we have been permitted to make in this portion of His Majesty's Empire.

We look forward with keen interest to seeing all which makes your city so venerated by the Hindus and renowned throughout the world. I shall be much pleased to transmit to the King-Emperor your gratifying acknowledgment of those blessings of peace and safety which you enjoy under his rule. We most sincerely reciprocate your kind wishes, and we both hope that this great city—the second city in the United Provinces—may ever flourish and prosper.

REPLY TO QUETTA MUNICIPALITY.

[His Majesty reached Quetta on 15th March, and in responding to the Quetta Municipal address, remarked :—]

Gentlemen,—The address which has just been read presents in very graphic language a story of which we may all feel proud. While thanking you heartily for your welcome to the Princess of Wales and myself, I congratulate you with equal heartiness on your achievements. We, who are familiar with the older and more slowly growing institutions of the West, are naturally struck with the rapid career of Quetta. You have mentioned the honoured name of Sandeman, who won the people of Baluchistan to the ways of peace. I doubt not that the traditions of that great man may inspire and direct you in your labours, and I can detect in your address two of his qualities—courage and hope.

We shall have opportunities during the next few days of seeing for ourselves the work which has been achieved within the short space of thirty years, and it will be my pleasing duty to inform the King-Emperor of the wonderful progress which has been made on this frontier of the Empire since he visited India. May every success and prosperity attend your useful labours. The concluding words of your address have greatly touched us, and we sincerely join your expressions of thankfulness for the blessings which Providence has bestowed upon us during our journey to and in India.

CHAMAN.

[In commiting new Colours to the 127th Baluch Light Infantry at Chaman, His Majesty said :—]

Colonel Even, Officers, Non-Commissioned officers and Men of the 127th Baluch Light Infantry,— Since the days when your Regiment was raised by Sir Charles Napier, more than 60 years ago, it has rendered gallant and devoted services to its Sovereign and Empire, not only in India but across the seas—in Africa, Burma and the Far East. The names of your compaigns are displayed on the Colours which I have great pleasure in presenting to you. They are a sign of your duty to your King-Emperor and Country, and also a record of those actions in which your predecessors have upheld the honour of the Regiment. For such reasons you rightly venerate them and upon them to take your oath of allegiance. May you ever be guided by the noble traditions which they betoken, and should you again be called to active service, may victory attend you. I am certain that the Colours will remain safe in your keeping.

REPLY TO KARACHI MUNICIPAL ADDRESS.

[On 17th March, His Majesty reached Karachi, where he made two speeches, one of these being, perhaps, the longest of all those he made during his tour. This was in reply to the Karachi Municipal address, which was in the following terms:—]

Gentlemen,—On behalf of the Princess of Wales and myself, I thank you for the welcome which you have given to us in this rising and prosperous seaport—the capital of Sind. Your progress is remarkable, even in an age of progress, but the figures which you have quoted and the strenuous policy of extending irrigation in Sind and the Punjab suggest the idea that vast developments await your City and Harbour in the immediate future.

I am very glad to have had an opportunity of seeing Karachi, for I am conscious of the fact that this place is destined to play an important part in the future of our Empire, and, if I may judge of the spirit of the inhabitants of Karachi from the sentiments expressed in your address, I have little fear that you and your successors in office will be able to grapple with the difficult question of development in a large and far-sighted manner. I have learnt with great pleasure that the Bombay Government has most courteously marked our visit to Karachi by the abolition of boat fees on the Indus. I do not know how far this wise act may directly affect Karachi, but I am proud that I should be associated with a concession which will at any rate benefit some of the people of Sind. Gentlemen, we wish you every prosperity in the great work which lies before the Municipality of Karachi.

Your concluding words of God-speed, for which we are both most grateful, remind us, alas ! that our visit to India is near its end. I can assure you and our other friends in all parts of this great and wonderful land that we leave India with feelings of gratitude and affection. We have seen and have learned much; we have seen enough to make India a living reality to us; enough to make us wish that we could see more, and to implant for ever in our hearts a sympathy and interest in all that affects our fellow subjects in India, of whatever creed or race.

Although our receptions everywhere were the scenes of brightness and splendour, and we have been greeted by thousands of cheerful and happy faces, we have not forgotten the hard lives led by those in the trying climates of the plains, and we know of the miseries which beset the patient, hardworking peasant when the rains do not come in due season. We are both sincerely thankful to have been privileged to visit India, and to have gained impressions which, with future study and observation, will enable me to try and understand some of the problems of British Administration, for I fully appreciate the advantage which a visit to this great continent must give to anyone in considering even the simplest Indian question.

Our journey has, in all parts of India, been most happy and delightful, thanks to the love and goodwill which have been evinced by all classes. We have been deeply impressed by that feeling of loyalty to the Crown and devotion to the person of the King-Emperor which has been displayed ever since we first set foot on Indian soil and we have been also greatly touched by the evident memories of affection towards my dear brother which still remain in the hearts of those with whom he was brought in contact during his stay in India some 16 years ago. In bidding India farewell, we can truly say that our visit has been to us an unending and unbroken series of happy and most instructive experiences.

UNVEILING VICTORIA STATUE AT KARACHI.

[The other speech he made there was before the unveiling of the Victoria statue at that town. In doing so, His Majesty said :—]

Gentlemen,—It is a great pleasure to the Princess of Wales and myself to take part in a ceremony which crowns the loyal and loving efforts of five long years, and it is our good fortune to have an opportunity of being associated with the people of Sind in this splendid tribute to our late beloved Queen-Empress. We have read the admirable pamphlet which describe the history of the memorial, and have noticed with interest the names of Mr. Giles and Mr. Moti Ram Adrani and others, to whose energy we owe so much. We have noticed, too, with special satisfaction that all classes in Sind have joined in raising this statue, which is fitly symbolised by figures of Peace and Justice. You do right to connect them with the memory of Queen Victoria, for she greatly desired that her Indian subjects should ever enjoy these blessings. I shall be happy to name the grounds on which we stand "The Queen's Lawn," and we both hope that this statue and the lawn around it may bring pleasure and recreation to endless generations. Gentlemen, we thank you for your parting words, and I shall not fail to convey to the King-Emperor and the Queen, the loyal expressions of the people of Sind. We were deeply touched by Bombay's affectionate welcome to the shores of India. On the eve of our departure we are equally impressed with Karachi's sympathy and good wishes.

SPEECH AT GUILDHALL, LONDON.

[To these speeches, has to be added the one that His Majesty made at the Guildhall Banquet, which was given him on the 17th May by the Corporation of London. Responding to the toast of "The Health of Her Majesty Queen Alexandra, Their Royal Highnesses, the Prince and the Princess of Wales, and the other Members of the Royal Family," His Majesty in a speech, which created a deep impression in England and in India, said:—]

My Lord Mayor, my Lords, Ladies and Gentlemen,—I wish to thank you, my Lord Mayor, with all my heart for the kind words in which you have proposed this toast, and I am much touched by the very kind and hearty reception which this distinguished company has given to it. My Lord Mayor, your feeling allusions to the Queen remind me how the recent sorrow of my dear mother was the one cloud which for a time overcast the brightness of our stay in India. On the other hand, one of our happiest experiences has been the glad and unexpected meeting with the King and Queen on our homeward voyage in the Mediterranean. With reference to your kind allusions to the other members of my family, I should like to say what a great pleasure it was to us that by a curious coincidence we met the Duke and Duchess of Connaught on their way to England after their very successful visit at South Africa. As the Lord Mayor has reminded us, we are all looking forward to the return of my cousin Prince Arthur, who, I believe, is expected to arrive at Liverpool to-morrow. I know that the country has followed with interest the incidents connected with his special mission to Japan and his subsequent visit to Canada. It must be very gratifying to his parents, as it is to us all, to hear that he has everywhere won golden opinions in carrying out his important duties. The Princess of Wales and I wish to express our deep appreciation of the hearty welcome we received on our arrival in England last week and again to-day here in the City of London. The seven months' absence has been to us a happy and interesting experience. Still, we rejoice to be at home again, and are thankful to God that he has spared us to return to our children and to those that are dear to us.

It is nearly five years ago that the Princess of Wales and I were entertained by the Lord Mayor and the City of London in this ancient hall on the termination of our memorable tour to our sister nations beyond the seas. We are met here to-day under similar circumstances and the conclusion of our visit to the great Indian Empire may, I think, be regarded as the completion of the mission originally entrusted to us by the King. It is a great satisfaction to us that we have been privileged to visit nearly every part of the British Empire. In thus accomplishing what has been the ambition of our lives, the Princess and I desire to express our sincere gratitude to the country for having enabled us to make this long voyage in such a fine vessel as the *Renown.* No less warmly do we thank the Government of India for the admirable arrangements for our railway journeys of nearly nine thousand miles, which were made with every possible consideration for our convenience and safety. It may perhaps interest you to know that we spent twenty-eight nights in our comfortable train. From the 16th of November, the day of our brilliant reception on landing at Bombay, until the moment of our departure from Karachi on the 19th of March, we were welcomed everywhere with a display of enthusiasm and affection which profoundly touched us, and the memory of which will never fade from our minds. We were still more impressed by the unmistakable proofs of genuine devotion and personal attachment to the King-Emperor. At every place we visited, where my dear father had been thirty years ago, the event was spoken of with the keenest interest and pride, not only by those who remembered seeing him, but also by the younger generation. Although we were welcomed everywhere by happy, holiday-making crowds which thronged the gaily-decorated streets, we did not forget the misery and poverty which, alas ! existed in certain districts afflicted by famines through which we passed. When at Gwalior I had an opportunity of inspecting a famine camp, and saw with sad interest, but with satisfaction, the excellent arrangements effectively carried out for mitigating the sufferings of upwards of 6,000 men, women, and children who were there employed, fed, and cared for.

Our visits to several of the great Feudatory States will always be reckoned among the happiest and most interesting of our experiences. We were received by the respective rulers and their peoples with the warmest enthusiasm, with all the gorgeousness and circumstance of old Indian customs, and by them entertained with magnificent hospitality. I enjoyed social intercourse with many of these great Princes, and I was impressed with their loyalty and personal allegience to the Crown, their nobility of mind, their chivalrous nature, and the great powers which they possess for doing good. I might mention that in several of these States the Imperial Service Troops are an important feature. They are raised, equipped and maintained by the Princes themselves, to be placed at our disposal in case of war. Though these States supply their own officers, these regiments are under the guidance and inspection of British Officers, and it is to be hoped that this excellent movement may be extended throughout all the Feudatory States. No one could possibly fail to be struck with the wonderful administration of India. Time did not permit of our leaving the beaten track for the interior of the country, and thereby gaining an insight into the machinery of that most efficient organisation, the government of a district. But we had opportunities of seeing at the head-quarters, of the Presidencies and of the differents Provinces the general and admirable working of the Civil Service. At the same time we realised that it is a mere handful of highly educated British officials, often living a hard and strenuous life, frequently separated from their fellow countrymen, and subject to the trials and discomforts of the plains, who are working hand in hand with representatives of the different races in the administration of enormous areas and in the government of millions of people. During the month of December, in the neighbourhood of Rawal Pindi, I had the pleasure of staying with Lord Kitchener in his camp of manœuvres, and witnessed operations on an extended scale between two Armies, numbering in all over 55,000 men, terminating in a review and march past of the largest force ever brought together in India in time of peace. I was struck with the general fitness and the splendid appearance of the British troops, with the physique and power of endurance of the Native Army and the dash of its Cavalry, while throughout the Army I found an earnest desire for increased efficiency and for readiness to take the field. I was specially glad to have this opportunity of being associated with our magnificent Army in India under such practical conditions. I am proud to say that during my tour I was able to inspect 143,000 troops. Having seen several colleges and other educational institutions in different parts of India, I gained some slight idea of the efforts that are being made to place within the reach of all classes a liberal education. Let me take as an example the great Mahomedan college and school at Aligarh, which is supported and controlled by the private enterprize of Mahomedan gentlemen from all parts of India. A residential system similar to that at Oxford and Cambridge has been adopted. At the same time athletics are not neglected, and in all schools and colleges there is much emulation in cricket and football. Undoubtedly, such institutions must materially affect the formation of character in future generations.

If I were asked to name any general impressions which I have formed during this exceptional but all too short experience, they would be that I have learnt to appreciate the fact that India cannot be regarded as one country. We talk casually of going to India. But the majority of us perhaps do not realise that it is a continent with an area equal to the whole of Europe, without Russia, containing a population of 300,000,000 of diverse races, languages and creeds, and many different grades of civilisation. I was struck with its immense size, its splendour, its numerous races, its varied climate, its snow-capped mountains, its boundless deserts, its mighty rivers, its architectural monuments, and its ancient traditions. I have realised the patience, the simplicity of life, the loyal devotion, and the religious spirit which characterise the Indian peoples. I know also their faith in the absolute justice and integrity of our rule. I cannot help thinking from all I have heard and seen that the task of governing India will be made the easier if we, on our part, infuse into it a wider element of sympathy. I will venture to predict that to such sympathy there will be an ever abundant and genuine response. May we not also hope for a still fuller measure of trust and confidence in our earnest desire and efforts to promote the well-being and to further the best interests of every class? In speaking of my impressions I should like very briefly to record a few of those scenes and incidents which will be to us of lasting value.

Would that I were able in any way to picture our arrival in Bombay amid the greetings and hearty acclamations of its cosmopolitan population dressed in every conceivable colour, and all beneath the clearest blue of an Eastern sky. Quitting Bombay in tropical heat, my thoughts carry me from there over hundreds of miles almost as far as from London to Constantinople, to the rigorous climate of the Khyber Pass. The Union Jack, floating over the fortress of Jamrud, reminds us that British protection is guaranteed to the caravans that pass twice a week to and from Afghanistan throughout this twenty-five miles of neutral territory. At Landi Kotal, the further entrance of the Pass, five British officers and a regiment of Afridis—that tribe which only a few years ago was fighting against us—now garrison this lonely outpost of our Indian Empire. To the historic stronghold of Ali Masjid came the leading Khans, each bringing offerings of goodwill in the shape of the pick of their flocks of sheep and the finest specimens of their honey. Contrast such wild and semi-civilised scenes with Delhi and Agra, those centres of artistic wealth and of priceless architectural monuments, for the preservation of which and the great care bestowed upon them universal thanks are due to the late Viceroy Lord Curzon. Imagine us next at Gwalior, and later on at Benares, making our public entry under conditions impossible in any other part of the world, mounted as we were on elephants gorgeously caparisoned and passing amid escorts and troops clothed and equipped in all the picturesqueness of mediæval pageantry. But among all these varied and striking impressions none have stirred our hearts as did the Ridge at Delhi and the grounds and ruins of the Lucknow Residency. They recalled with vivid reality those glorious heroes and those thrilling deeds which will for ever make sacred the story of the Indian Mutiny. I think you will all be interested to know that Colonel Bonham, one of the few survivors of the siege of Lucknow, is present here among us to-day. Although he was wounded three times during the siege, I am glad to say he is still fit and well, and was good enough to act as our guide when we were at Lucknow in December last. The new year saw us in Calcutta, the capital of India, and the second largest city of the British Empire, where our reception was most cordial and sympathetic. Here I had the satisfaction of laying the foundation stone of the Queen Victoria Memorial Hall, a great and national memorial—the inception of which is chiefly due to Lord Curzon—to be a treasure-house of relics and records of the life and reign of our late beloved Sovereign, whose memory is held in loving veneration by every race throughout the Continent of India.

If time permitted I should like to dwell upon Burma, so different as it is from India in the nature of its people and in its social characteristics, to speak of the famous Golden Pagoda at Rangoon, of the interesting sights at Mandalay, and of three delightful days spent on the great River Irrawaddi. Let us change the scene to Madras and its historic associations, so closely connected with the foundation of our Indian Empire. Let us pass thence through the hot plains of Southern India, journeying northwards through Benares, the metropolis of Hinduism, with its sacred river and famous shrines, until at length we re-enter the region of frost and snows at Quetta, with its outpost at Chaman, another gate-way in that wild and mountainous district which constitutes our North-West Frontier of India. Leaving Quetta, we retrace our steps through that triumph of engineering skill, the railroad through the Bolan Pass, and descending from an altitude of 5,500 ft., we pass through the burning plains of Sind and reach Karachi, the rapidly-growing port of that province. And here we bid farewell to the country where for many months we had found a second home and for whose people we shall preserve a lasting affection. But these are mere first impressions. I am fully aware how impossible it is to gain accurate and intimate knowledge of so vast a country by a visit of only four and a half months. Yet I would strongly suggest to those who are interested in the great questions which surround the India of to-day to go there and learn as much as is possible by personal observation on the spot. I cannot but think that every Briton who treads the soil of India is assisting towards a better understanding with the Mother Country, helping to break down prejudice, to dispel misapprehension and to foster sympathy and brotherhood. Thus he will not only strengthen the old ties but create new ones and so, please God! secure a better understanding and a closer union of hearts between the Mother Country and her Indian Empire.

Part II.

SPEECHES

DELIVERED IN INDIA

DURING THE

Coronation Durbar Tour.

REPLY TO
THE ADDRESS OF THE PEOPLE OF ADEN.

[Replying to the address of welcome presented to him by the inhabitants of Aden, on 28th November 1911, His Imperial Majesty the King-Emperor replied as follows :—]

I thank you on behalf of the Queen-Empress and myself for your loyal Address and for the hearty welcome, which the Community of Aden has extended to us. No more fitting spot could have been chosen, on which to give expression to these sentiments of personal attachment and devotion than here beneath the statue of my beloved grand-mother, Queen Victoria. It is a source of sincere pleasure to us to revisit your famous port and to assure ourselves of its continued promise and prosperity. Situated on the threshold of India, and forming a connecting link between Great Britain and Australia, Aden is an object of peculiar interest to the whole of the British Empire and the responsibilities which you as citizens of the Empire are called upon to assume become year by year of increasing importance. I have learnt with great satisfaction of the steady expansion of your trade and I trust that the investigations which are now in course of completion will give you the improved and adequate water supply upon which your health and well-being so largely depend. The reclamations which have been made upon the sea face will afford the space which you require for the development of your town and I rejoice at the decision to reserve a portion of them for a recreation ground. We thank you for your good wishes and prayers on our behalf and you may rest assured that we shall ever feel the warmest interest in your welfare and prosperity.

REPLY TO THE BOMBAY CORPORATION.

[On their arrival at Bombay, Their Majesties were presented with an address of welcome by the Bombay Corporation on 2nd December 1911, to which His Majesty made the following reply, which will live long in the memories of the Indian nation :—]

"You have rightly said that I am no stranger among you, and I can heartily respond that I feel myself no stranger in your beautiful City. Six years ago I arrived, indeed, as a new-comer, but the recollection of your cordial and sympathetic greeting is still fresh in my memory. The wondrous aspect disclosed by the approach to your shores, the first glimpse of the palms rising as it were from the bosom of the sea, have not been forgotten, and have lost none of their fascination for me. From Bombay I set forth in 1905, encouraged by your affectionate welcome, to traverse at any rate a part of this vast country, and to strive to gain some knowledge of its people. Such knowledge as I acquired could not but deepen my sympathy with all races and creeds, and when through the lamented death of my beloved father I was called to the Throne of my ancestors, one of my first and most earnest desires was to revisit my good subjects in India. (Cheers.)

It is with feelings of no common emotion that I find myself here again to-day with the Queen-Empress at my side—(applause)—and that desire fulfilled. And I come with a heart full of gratitude that the anxiety due to a threatened scarcity in certain areas of the Presidency has, thanks to favourable and opportune rains, been happily dispelled, and that there is every prospect of your land being blessed with a good spring harvest. (Cheers.)

Your eloquent Address has recalled to me that Bombay was once the dowry of a British Queen. As such Humphrey Cook took it over 250 years ago, a mere fishing village. You, gentlemen, and your forerunners have made it a jewel of the British Crown. (Applause.) I see again with joy the rich setting of its beautiful and stately buildings. I note also the less conspicuous, but also more profitable, improvements lately effected; but above all, I recognise with pride your efforts to heighten what must always be the supreme lustre of such a jewel as this, the peace, happiness, and prosperity of all classes of the citizens. (Cheers.)

From my heart I thank you for the generous reception accorded to the Queen-Empress and myself to-day. We earnestly pray that God's blessing may rest upon our Indian Empire, and that peace and prosperity may be ever vouchsafed to its people. (Cheers.)

[His Majesty having read his speech, Lady Mehta, in a Parsee dress, presented a beautiful bouquet of pink and white roses and lilies tied with silk of the same colour to Her Majesty. The members of the Bombay Corporation were then presented to the King, who acknowledged their salutations with salutes.]

REPLY TO INDIAN PEOPLE'S ADDRESS.

[Their Imperial Majesties arrived in Delhi on 7th December, amidst scenes of great enthusiasm, and the Hon'ble Mr. Jenkins, as Vice-President of the Imperial Legislative Council, presented an address of welcome to them "on behalf of the peoples of British India." In that address it was stated that "loyalty to the Sovereign is pre-eminently an Indian virtue, inculcated by sages and religious preceptors from time immemorial, and in all Your Imperial Majesty's wide dominions Your Imperial Majesty has no subjects more loyal and faithful than the inhabitants of British India." His Majesty the King-Emperor in reply said :—]

In the name of the Queen-Empress and on my own behalf I heartily thank you for your loyal and dutiful Address, the words of which have deeply touched us. They recall those countless messages of affectionate devotion with which India in common with all parts of my dominions greeted us on our Coronation in England and which have been repeated by all classes and creeds of my

Indian subjects since our arrival in your country.

I know from my Governor-General what strength and support he receives from the wise experience of the Members of his Legislative Council, the chosen representatives of British India. I much appreciate the welcome you offer us on behalf of its peoples. Rest assured that there is no wish nearer to our hearts than that, in the words of your Address, the Indian Empire may continue steadily to advance in the ways of peace, prosperity and contentment.

SPEECH
AT THE ALL-INDIA MEMORIAL, DELHI.

[The greatest event of the second day of Their Majesties' arrival at Delhi—8th December 1911—was the unveiling of the All-India Memorial Tablet to the late King Edward VII., in the centre of a well-laid out garden, which was specially created on the Delhi Maidan between the Fort and the Jumma Masjid. The tablet is to form the foundation of the large bronze statue that is to be set up at the spot. In the presence of a large concourse of people, Feudatory Princes, Heads of Administrations, high officials, and other subscribers to the Fund, Lord Hardinge stepped forward to read an address, in which he said that "in the statue that is to adorn this pedestal will be enshrined a lasting pledge of the gratitude of the many millions of your Indian people for the peace, justice and prosperity that prevailed during the late King-Emperor's all too short but strenuous reign." His Imperial Majesty, in reply, said:—]

The Address which you have just read has touched my heart and awakened memories of what we all, and I most of all, owe to my dear father, the late King-Emperor. He was the first of my House to visit India, and it was by his command that I came six short years ago to this great and wonderful land. Alas! little did we then think how soon we should have to mourn his loss.

You tell me that this Memorial represents the contributions, not only of a few who may have had the privilege of personal acquaintance with my father, but of thousands of his and my people in India. I am glad to know that the deep and abiding concern which he felt for India has met with so warm a response from the hearts of her children.

I rejoice to think that this statue will stand a noble monument on a beautiful and historic site to remind generations yet unborn of your loyal affection and of his sympathy and trust, sentiments which, please God, always will be traditional between India and the members of my House.

[His Imperial Majesty, accompanied by the Queen-Empress, then advanced to the base of the pedestal and unveiled the Tablet. The assembled troops gave a Royal Salute; the Massed Bands struck up the National Anthem; and the entire assembly rose. The Saluting

Battery stationed near the Water Gate fired a Salute of 101 guns. The senior Member of the Committee advanced and tendered to the Governor-General a miniature of the Memorial, which His Imperial Majesty graciously accepted.]

ADDRESS TO BRITISH AND INDIAN REGIMENTS.

[On 11th December 1911, an imposing and picturesque ceremony took place at Delhi at which His Majesty presented new Colours to seven British and two Indian Regiments. His Majesty in presenting Colours to the Indian Regiments said :—]

For many ages the Colours of a Regiment were its rallying point in battle. To-day they remain an emblem of duty, the outward symbol of allegiance to God and Empire, and as a record of past victories. As such I commit these new Colours to your keeping. May they recall the old soldiers' gallant deeds of the past and kindle within their younger comrades zeal for fresh achievements and for devoted service to the Crown. Religious freedom is now your birth-right. Consecrate these Colours, as you will recognise in them a sacred trust. In your hands they are safe. Under their inspiration you will, I know, ever maintain untarnished the proud record of your forefathers.

[Addressing the British Regiments, His Majesty the King-Emperor said :—]

I am very glad to have this opportunity of giving new Colours to so many of my Battalions while I am in India. The presentation of Colours is a solemn occasion in the history of a Regiment, for you then bid farewell to the old Flag which bears upon it the record of past achievements, receiving in return a new Flag upon which it lies with you to inscribe the names of future victories. Recalling with pride the deeds of those who have gone before you, look forward with hope into the coming days. Remember these are no common flags which I am committing to your keeping. A Colour is a sacred ensign ever by its inspiration, though no longer by its presence, a rallying point in battle. It is the emblem of duty, the outward sign of your allegiance to God, your Sovereign and country, to be looked up to, to be venerated and to be passed down untarnished to succeeding generations.

To Face Page 117.

THE PEOPLE'S THRONE: HIS MAJESTY PROCLAIMING BOONS THROUGH THE VICEROY.

DURBAR OPENING ADDRESS.

[On 12th December 1911, at 11-30 A.M., Their Imperial Majesties drove from the Camp to the Amphitheatre, with escorts of British and Indian Cavalry, a Battery of Horse Artillery and the Imperial Cadet Corps. They were greeted there with a Salute of 101 guns. The Governor-General of India, His Excellency Lord Hardinge, received them and conducted them to their Thrones. The Durbar having been opened, His Majesty the King-Emperor graciously addressed his people. His Majesty said:—]

It is with genuine feelings of thankfulness and satisfaction that I stand here to-day among you. This year has been to the Queen-Empress and myself one of many great ceremonies and of an unusual though happy burden of toil, but in spite of time and distance, the grateful recollections of our last visit to India have drawn us again to the land which we then learned to love, and we started with bright hopes on our long journey to revisit the country in which we had already met the kindness of a home. In doing so, I have fulfilled the wish expressed in my message of last

July, to announce to you in person my Coronation, celebrated on the 22nd of June, in Westminster Abbey, when by the Grace of God the Crown of my forefathers was placed on my head with solemn form and ancient ceremony. By my presence with the Queen-Empress I am also anxious to show our affection for the loyal Princes and faithful peoples of India and how dear to our hearts is the welfare and happiness of the Indian Empire. It is, moreover, my desire that those who could not be present at the solemnity of the Coronation should have the opportunity of taking part in its commemoration at Delhi.

It is a sincere pleasure and gratification to myself and to the Queen-Empress to behold this vast assemblage and in it my Governors and trusted officials, my great Princes, the representatives of the peoples and deputations from the Military Forces of my Indian dominions. I shall receive in person with heartfelt satisfaction the homage and allegiance which they loyally desire to render. I am deeply impressed with the thought that a spirit of sympathy and affectionate goodwill unites Princes and people with me on this historical occasion. In token of these sentiments I have desired to commemorate the event of my Coronation by certain marks of my special favour and consideration, and these I will later on to-day cause to be announced by my Governor-General to this Assembly. Finally, I rejoice to have this opportunity of renewing in my own person those assurances which have been given by my revered predecessors of the maintenance of your rights and privileges and of my earnest concern for your welfare, peace and contentment. May the Divine favour of Providence watch over my people and assist me in my utmost endeavour to promote their happiness and prosperity. To all present feudatories and subjects I tender our loving greeting.

[Thereafter were announced the Coronation boons, printed herein as Appendix.]

SPEECH ON THE TRANSFER OF THE CAPITAL.

[At the conclusion of the great Durbar of 12th December, 1911, His Majesty the King-Emperor made the following announcements regarding the transfer of the Imperial Capital to Delhi and the modification of the Bengal Partition :—]

We are pleased to announce to our people that on the advice of our Ministers tendered after consultation with our Governor-General in Council, we have decided upon the transfer of the seat of the Government of India from Calcutta to the ancient Capital of Delhi, and simultaneously, and as a consequence of that transfer, the creation at as early a date as possible of a Governorship for the Presidency of Bengal, of a new Lieutenant-Governorship in Council administering the areas of Behar, Chota Nagpur and Orissa, and of a Chief Commissionership of Assam, with such administrative changes and redistribution of boundaries as our Governor-General in Council, with the approval of our Secretary of State for India in Council, may in due course determine. It is our earnest desire that these changes may conduce to the better administration of India and the greater prosperity and happiness of our beloved people.

REPLY TO MADRAS ADDRESS.

[His Majesty the King-Emperor was on the 13th December 1911, presented with an Address by a deputation from Madras headed by Mr. A. E. Lawson C.I.E., Sheriff of Madras, and Editor, *Madras Mail*, and in reply to the Address, His Majesty said :—]

I thank you heartily for your loyal and dutiful Address of Welcome to the Queen-Empress and myself on behalf of the people of the Presidency of Madras. We are deeply moved by the loyal feelings which have inspired the inhabitants of the oldest Province in our Indian Dominions, numbering over forty million people, to unite in giving so cordial a demonstration of their attachment to our Throne and person. The great volume containing signatures representing all the different races, castes and creeds of Southern India will be ever treasured by us as a precious testimony of your loving welcome.

We appreciate highly the terms in which you have referred to the occasion of our present visit to India and your affectionate remembrance of our stay in Madras in 1906. We have not forgotten the hearty greeting which was then extended to us, and it is a source of deep regret that the limited time available has not permitted us to accede to your wishes and to include a visit to your famous city.

I have heard with profound gratification your kindly allusions to the sympathetic interests which the great Queen Victoria and my beloved father and mother displayed in the prosperity of their Indian Empire. I need not assure you that I share those feelings, and that the welfare and prosperity of my Indian subjects will ever be objects of my earnest solicitude.

REPLY TO DELHI MUNICIPAL ADDRESS.

[On the 13th of December 1911, an important and influential deputation from the Delhi Municipal Council waited upon His Majesty the King-Emperor and presented an Address of Welcome. Mr. Barron, President of the Delhi Municipal Committee, headed it. The members were presented to the King-Emperor and His Majesty in replying to the Address said :—]

The Queen-Empress and I thank you most heartily for the kind sentiments of welcome and goodwill to which your Address gives expression. A few months ago we feared lest the occasion of our visit to India should be marked by a serious scarcity owing to a period of unusual drought, thus causing grievous calamity to the large majority of my Indian people, whose prosperity so closely depends upon an abundant rainfall and upon the produce of agriculture. I am thankful that the scarcity has been restricted in extent, and that owing to better communications and the extension of irrigation, famine to-day is no longer the dread scourge of past generations.

I am glad to know that in other directions the agricultural position of India has improved. The cultivator has always been patient, laborious and skilful, though his methods have been based upon tradition. Latterly, the resources of science have been brought to bear upon agriculture, and have demonstrated, in a very short time, the great results that can be secured by its application, not only in the actual improvement of the land but in dealing with the diseases of live stock, and also with those insect-pests which are such formidable enemies of the tiller of the soil. If the system of co-operation can be introduced and utilised to the full, I foresee a great and glorious future for the agricultural interests of this country.

We greatly appreciate the successful efforts made to beautify and prepare your City for our visit. At the same time, I know how during the past twenty years you have not neglected sanitary reform. Steady progress with your drainage system has had most happy results, and the supply of pure water which you have secured has fully justified its heavy cost in the immunity thereby given from cholera and other epidemic diseases. The unusual freedom from malaria which Delhi has enjoyed this year is, I understand, to be ascribed largely to the clearance and drainage of the Bela, by which a jungle swamp has been converted into an extensive Park.

I most earnestly trust that these lessons may be more universally understood and utilised to ensure the better health and greater safety of my Indian subjects. The remedy for protection from those terrible visitations of plague, malaria and cholera must be sought in the action of the people themselves and their leaders, in cordial co-operation with the scientific efforts of the authorities. Considerable progress has been made by research and by the study of local conditions as to the cause of these scourges, but much remains to be done; above all, in the education of the masses, teaching them to understand and adopt precautions dictated by elementary hygiene and domestic sanitation for their protection and welfare.

We have looked forward with keen pleasure to the prospect of re-visiting your ancient and famous City, which, as your Address reminds us, has been the scene of events memorable in the history of this country, and some of them intimately associated with my House and Throne. In the future it will be bound to us by yet closer ties. The traditions of your City invest it with a peculiar charm. The relics of the dynasties of bygone ages that meet the eye on every side, the splendid palaces and temples which have resisted the destroying hand of time, all these witness to a great and illustrious past.

In seeking a more central spot for the seat of the Government of India these traditions and characteristics conduced in no small degree to the decision which I have so recently announced, that from this time forth Delhi shall be the Capital of our Indian Empire.

At the same time, I wish to bear testimony to the care with which the Government of the Punjab, during the fifty years since Delhi was incorporated in that Province, have developed this beautiful City, while doing their utmost to preserve its historic monuments and thus preparing the City of Delhi for its restoration to its former proud position of the Capital of the Indian Empire.

The change will necessitate considerable administrative re-arrangements, but I am assured that the Imperial City may anticipate from the Imperial Government care for its ancient monuments and a solicitude for its material development by no means less than the Provincial City of Delhi has in the past received from the Provincial Government.

I pray that this Empire, of which Delhi is now the Capital, may ever stand for peace and progress, justice and prosperity, and that it may add to the traditions of your City still brighter chapters of greatness and glory.

INAUGURATION OF THE NEW CAPITAL OF INDIA.

[On 15th December 1911, a ceremony took place at Delhi, at the conclusion of which Their Imperial Majesties laid the first stones of the new Capital of India. The place selected was in the Government of India Camp, which has been decided to be the centre of the Imperial Delhi that is to be. The Heralds and the whole of the Local Government and Administrations were in attendance, also the Ruling Chiefs and the Coronation Durbar Heralds and Trumpeters, with a Guard of Honour and Escorts. Their Majesties, on arrival, were received by the Governor-General and the Members of the Executive Council. A Royal Salute was fired. The Governor-General then made a short speech, which is printed as an Appendix and His Imperial Majesty replying thereto, said :—]

It is a matter of supreme satisfaction to the Queen-Empress and myself that it has been possible for us, before leaving Delhi, to lay the first stones of the Imperial Capital, which will arise from where we now stand. This is the first step

To Face Page 129.

STATE ENTRY : THE ROYAL PROCESSION AT THE PAVILION IN FORT.

to give the material effect to the important announcement which it was my pleasure to make on that magnificent and, to us, deeply impressive occasion of my Coronation Durbar three days ago.

I earnestly hope that the anticipation of the beneficial and far-reaching results from the great changes now to be effected may be amply fulfilled, securing to India improved administration and to its people increased happiness and prosperity. It is my desire that the planning and designing of the public buildings to be erected will be considered with the greatest deliberation and care, so that the new creation may be in every way worthy of this ancient and beautiful city.

May God's blessing rest upon the work which is so happily inaugurated to-day.

[After the speech His Majesty the King-Emperor laid one stone and the Queen-Empress another, and both then returned in royal procession to the dais. The Heralds announced, first in English and then in Urdu, His Majesty's command that the foundation had been well and truly laid. A fanfare of trumpets followed, and Sir Louis Dane called for three cheers for Their Imperial Majesties in the new Capital. These were heartily responded to and the assembly separated.]

REPLY TO
THE CALCUTTA CORPORATION ADDRESS.

[The following speech was delivered by His Majesty on 4th January in reply to the address of the Calcutta Corporation:—]

I thank you warmly on behalf of the Queen-Empress and myself for the assurance of the loyalty on the part of the Corporation and the citizens of the City of Calcutta, to which your address gives expression.

We are deeply touched by your kindly reference to my beloved Father's stay in your city and by your affectionate allusion to our own visit here six years ago. We can never forget the cordial welcome given us on that occasion, while the sympathetic interest in your Indian Empire, which the first sight of this great city inspired has in no way abated. It is a source of great pleasure to us to revisit Calcutta and see for ourselves evidence of your progress and prosperity.

The changes in the administration of India, resulting from the announcement made by me at the great Durbar at Delhi, will affect, to a certain extent, Calcutta. But your city must always remain the premier city of India. Its population, its importance as a commercial centre and great emporium of trade, its splendid historic traditions all combine to invest Calcutta with a unique character, which should preserve to it a pre-eminent position. At the same time, the status of the Province, of which Calcutta is the Capital, has been enhanced by the creation of a Presidency of Bengal, and I feel confident that under the wise administration of a Governor in Council, the new Presidency will enjoy increased prosperity with the blessings of tranquillity and order.

I know that you cherish ambitions that India will one day become a great manufacturing as well as an agricultural country. I have watched with keen interest the progress of your business enterprises, and I trust that the success which has attended your commercial energy will attract more and more of the youth of this country to regard commerce as a distinguished and honourable profession.

I thank you for your kind wishes and prayers. It shall ever be Our earnest endeavour to promote the welfare of Our Indian Empire and We fervently hope that the years, as they pass, will ever strengthen the feeling of warm attachment that exists between my House and my Indian people.

REPLY TO THE CALCUTTA UNIVERSITY

[The following is the reply of His Majesty the King-Emperor to the Address presented by the Senate of the Calcutta University on the 6th Jan. :—]

I recall with pleasure the occasion on which, six years ago, I received from the University of Calcutta the Honorary Degree of a Doctor of Law, and I am glad to have an opportunity to-day of showing my deep and earnest interest in the higher education of India. It is to the Universities of India that I look to assist in that gradual union and fusion of the culture and aspiration of Europeans and Indians on which the future well-being of India so greatly depends. I have watched with sympathy the measures that from time to time have been taken by the Universities of India to extend the scope and raise the standards of instruction. Much remains to be done. No University is now-a-days complete unless it is equipped with teaching faculties in all the more important branches of the sciences and the arts, and unless it provides ample opportunities for research. You have to conserve the ancient learning and simultaneously to push forward Western science. You have also to build up character, without which learning is of little value. You say that you recognise your great responsibilities. I bid you God-speed in the work that is before you. Let your ideals be high and your efforts to pursue them unceasing and, under Providence you will succeed.

Six years ago I sent from England to India a message of sympathy. To-day in India I give to India the watchword of hope. On every side I trace the signs and stirrings of new life. Education has given you hope; and through better and higher education you will build up higher and better hopes. The announcement was made at Delhi by my command that my Governor-General in Council will allot large sums for the expansion and improvement of education in India. It is my wish that there may be spread over the land a network of schools and colleges, from which will go forth loyal and manly and useful citizens, able to hold their own in industries and agriculture and all the vocations in life. And it is my wish, too, that the homes of my Indian subjects may be brightened and their labour sweetened by the spread of knowledge with what follows in its train, a higher level of thought, of comfort, and of health. It is through education that my wish will be fulfilled, and the cause of education in India will ever be very close to my heart.

It is gratifying to me to be assured of your devotion to myself and to my House, of your desire to strengthen the bonds of union between Great Britain and India, and of your appreciation of the advantages which you enjoy under British Rule. I thank you for your loyal and dutiful address.

REPLY TO THE BENGAL LEGISLATIVE COUNCIL.

[At Princep's Ghaut on the 8th January the Hon. Mr. F. E. Slacke read an Address on behalf of the Bengal Council, dwelling upon the results of the Royal visit, and expressing the hope that Their Imperial Majesties would revisit India. The King-Emperor replied as follows :—]

The Queen-Empress and I are deeply moved by the words of your Address, and they are no empty words. They have been amply and visibly proved by the enthusiastic reception accorded to us on our arrival here, and, no less by the affectionate demonstrations by which we have been greeted everywhere and by all classes in Calcutta and its surrounding neighbourhood. For the remainder of our lives we shall remember with feelings of pride and emotion the stirring experience of these past eight days. We shall recall the warm-hearted greeting extended to us on our arrival in your Capital, and the sight of the patient and sympathetic multitudes which had assembled from all parts of the Province to testify to their loyalty, and I am gratified by the assurances given in your Address that these outward proofs of allegiance and affection reflect the general sentiments of your fellow-subjects throughout the length and breadth of North-Eastern India.

Nor shall We forget the striking scenes and brilliant displays which have been so successfully organised and carried out to celebrate Our visit. The people of Bengal offer us as a farewell gift their "overflowing love and gratitude." You may rest assured that the Queen-Empress and I could ask for nothing more precious to us and to our children. We take it back to them to be cherished by them as a priceless heirloom. Our hearts are too full to express adequately the gratitude for all you have done to welcome us and to make us at home amongst you.

In bidding you farewell, the Queen-Empress and I fervently pray that all my subjects in Bengal, of whatever race or creed, united by the ties of sympathy and brotherly love, may, under Divine guidance, ever strive towards the advancement of their common happiness, contentment and general well-being.

REPLY TO THE BOMBAY LEGISLATIVE COUNCIL.

[His Imperial Majesty in reply to the Address presented by the members of the Bombay Legislative Council on 10th January, on the eve of his departure from India said :—]

I thank you sincerely on behalf of the Queen-Empress and myself for the kind and generous terms of the address of farewell, which you present in the name of the people of the Bombay Presidency.

The cordial welcome which we received on our arrival in your capital was the prelude to that display of warm-hearted loyalty which has characterised every stage of our progress during the past five weeks; and now we have listened with mingled feelings of gratification and sorrow to your touching words of farewell and God-speed.

Your hopeful forecasts as to the benefits which India will derive from this visit deepen our thankfulness at having accomplished the earnest wish of our heart. It has given me infinite pleasure to be once more among my faithful subjects in India and the Queen-Empress and I have been touched beyond words by the genuine love and devotion towards us, which we feel have entered into the spirit of the people. Our one and only cause of regret during these past happy weeks has been our inability to stay longer in this country and to visit the ancient Presidency of Madras and the States of the many Chiefs who have offered us their generous hospitality. On leaving the shores of India we carry lasting memories of experiences made pleasant by every means that thoughtful care and affectionate regard could devise. We fervently trust that our visit may by God's Grace conduce to the general good of the people of this great continent. Their interests and well-being will always be as near and as dear to me as those of the millions of my subjects in other quarters of the globe. It is a matter of intense satisfaction to me to realise how all classes and creeds have joined together in the true-hearted welcome which has been so universally accorded to us. Is it not possible that the same unity and concord may for the future govern the daily relations of their private and public life? The attainment of this would indeed be to us a happy outcome of our visit to India.

To you, the representatives of Bombay, who have greeted us so warmly on our arrival and departure, I deliver this our message of loving farewell to the Indian Empire.

May the Almighty ever assist me and my successors in the earnest endeavour to promote its welfare and to secure to it the blessings of prosperity and peace.

MESSAGE TO MR. ASQUITH.

[His Majesty the King telegraphed as follows to Mr. Asquith on the 10th instant:—]

Before leaving India on our homeward voyage, I am sure that you, as the head of my Government, will be glad to know that from all sources, private and public, I gather that my highest hopes have been realised and that the success of our visit has exceeded all expectations, not only in Bombay, Delhi and Calcutta, but in every other part of the country where the Queen and I have been. All classes, races and creeds have united in receiving us with unmistakable signs of enthusiasm and affection.

The magnificent display at the Durbar was the outcome of wise and well-considered plans, brilliantly carried out, through the untiring efforts of the Viceroy and those working under him.

During our pleasant visit to the Viceroy, all Calcutta combined in doing everything possible for our comfort and enjoyment. I rejoice that, thanks to the mutual confidence between me and my people at Home, I have been enabled to fulfil the wish of my heart. This satisfaction will be still greater if time proves that our visit has conduced to the lasting good of India and of the Empire at large.

MESSAGE TO THE VICEROY.

[H. E. the Viceroy telegraphed to His Imperial Majesty the King-Emperor on the 13th instant:—]

With humble duty, on leaving Indian waters all India wishes Your Imperial Majesties God-speed on your journey and prays for your safe and happy arrival in England. Your Imperial Majesties' visit to India will always be treasured by your loyal Indian subjects as a priceless incident in the history of India.

[His Imperial Majesty the King-Emperor on the 14th instant replied as follows :—]

Before leaving Indian waters the Queen and I desire again to acknowledge with sincere gratitude all that you have done for us during our most happy and never-to-be-forgotten stay in India, and at the same time to congratulate you heartily upon the admirable manner in which everything in connection with our visit was planned and carried out.

REPLY TO THE NATIONAL CONGRESS.

[The first resolution passed by the Calcutta Congress of 1911 was one of profound homage and heartiest welcome to Their Majesties tendered through H. E. the Viceroy. The following gracious reply was vouchsafed through the same channel :—]

Dear Sir,—With reference to your letter of the 26th December forwarding copy of a resolution of welcome to Their Gracious Majesties, I write to inform you that the resolution was duly telegraphed to Their Imperial Majesties. In reply I am commanded to convey to you the high appreciation of the King-Emperor and the Queen-Empress of the dutiful and loyal message of welcome sent to them by the Indian National Congress. If the visit to India is productive of lasting benefit to this vast land and its peoples Their Imperial Majesties will still more rejoice that it was possible for them to fulfil the great wish of their hearts.—J. H. Du Boulay, Private Secretary to the Governor-General.

To Face Page 144.

NATIVE PRINCES PAYING HOMAGE TO HIS MAJESTY.

Appendix A.

SPEECH OF HER MAJESTY THE QUEEN-EMPRESS.

REPLY TO INDIAN LADIES' ADDRESS.

[On the morning of 9th December 1911, the Queen-Empress held a Reception of Maharanis and other distinguished Indian ladies, at a purdah party in the Queen's Drawing Room at the King's Camp, Delhi. Among those thus honoured was the young daughter of the Rajah of Vizianagram. The Duchess of Devonshire and the Countess of Shaftesbury were in attendance. An Address was read by Lady Hardinge on behalf of the Indian ladies and a handsome jewel was presented, as a souvenir of the most unique and interesting occasion. Her Majesty, in reply, said :—]

The beautiful spirit of your welcome affects me deeply, and I trust that those who meet me here to-day will themselves accept and convey to the sisterhood of this Empire my warm thanks for their gentle greetings and sincere homage. I desire to assure you all of my ever-increasing solicitude for the happiness and welfare of those who live "within the walls." The pages of history have set forth what splendid influences for good can be brought to bear in their homes by the women of India, and the annals of its noble races are coloured by acts of devoted fealty and magnificent service as fruits of the lessons instilled by mothers in the hearts and minds of their children.

I have learnt with deep satisfaction the evolution which is gradually but surely taking place amongst the inmates of the *Purdah*, and I am convinced that you all desire to encourage education amongst your children so that they may grow up fitted to become useful and cultivated companions to their future husbands.

The jewel you have given me will ever be very precious in my eyes, and whenever I wear it, though thousands of miles of land and sea separate us, my thoughts will fly to the homes of India and create again and again this happy meeting and recall the love your tender hearts have yielded me. Your jewel shall pass to future generations as an Imperial heirloom and always stand as a token of the first meeting of an English Queen with the ladies of India.

I thank you for your congratulations and for the good wishes expressed by you towards the King-Emperor and myself, and join my prayers to yours for the strength, unity and well-being of the Empire.

Appendix B.

CORONATION BOONS.

HIS MAJESTY'S GRACIOUS COMMANDS.

[At the conclusion of the gracious speech of His Majesty the King-Emperor, on 12th December 1911, on the opening of the great and historic Durbar, Lord Hardinge rose and read His Majesty's Gracious Commands, which were received with continued cheering. He said :—]

A GRANT FOR EDUCATION.

To all to whom these presents may come by the command of His Most Excellent Majesty George V., by the Grace of God, King of the United Kingdom of Great Britain and Ireland and of the British Dominions beyond the Seas, Defender of the Faith and Emperor of India, I, his Governor-General do hereby declare and notify the grants, concessions, reliefs, and benefactions, which His Imperial Majesty has been graciously pleased to bestow upon this glorious and memorable occasion. Humbly and dutifully submissive to His Most

Gracious Majesty's will and pleasure, the Government of India have resolved, with the approval of His Imperial Majesty's Secretary of State, to acknowledge the predominant claims of educational advancement and have decided, in recognition of a very commendable demand, to act themselves, to make education in India as accessible and wide as possible. With this purpose it is proposed to devote at once Rs. 50 lakhs for the promotion of truly popular education, and it is the firm intention of the Government to add to the grant now announced further grants in future years on a generous scale.

CONCESSIONS TO THE ARMY.

Graciously recognising the signal and faithful services of his forces by land and seas, the King-Emperor has charged me to announce the award of half a month's pay of rank to all Non-commissioned Officers and men and Reservists, both of his British Army in India and his Indian Army, to the equivalent ranks of the Royal Indian Marine and to all permanent employees of Departmental or Combatant Establishments paid from the Military Estimates, whose pay may not exceed the sum of Rs. 50 monthly.

Furthermore, His Imperial Majesty has been graciously pleased to ordain that from henceforth the loyal Native Officers, men and Reservists of his Indian Army, shall be eligible for the grant of the Victoria Cross for valour, that the membership of the Order of British India shall be increased during the decade following this, His Imperial Majesty's Coronation Durbar, by 52 appointments in the First Class, and that in mark of these historic ceremonies, fifteen new appointments in the First Class and nineteen new appointments in the Second Class shall forthwith be made. That from henceforth Indian Officers of the Frontier Militia Corps and the Military Police shall be deemed eligible for admission to the aforesaid Order, that special grants of land or assessments or remissions of Land Revenue, as the case may be, shall now be conferred on certain Native Officers of His Imperial Majesty's Indian Army, who may be distinguished for long and honourable service, and that the special allowances now assigned for three years only to the widows of the deceased members of the Indian Order of Merit shall, with effect from the date of this Durbar, hereafter be continued to all such widows until death or marriage.

Graciously appreciating the devoted and successful labours of his Civil Service, His Imperial Majesty has commanded me to declare the grant of half a month's pay to all permanent servants in the civil employ of Government, whose pay may not exceed the sum of Rs. 50 monthly.

BADGES AND PENSIONS.

Further, it is His Imperial Majesty's Gracious behest that all persons to whom may have been or hereafter may be granted the titles of Dewan Bahadur, Sirdar Bahadur, Khan Bahadur, Rai Bahadur, Khan Sahib, Rai Sahib or Rao Sahib shall receive distinctive Badges as a symbol of respect and honour, and that on all holders present or to come of the venerable titles of Mahamahopadyaya and Shams-ul-Ulma shall be conferred some annual pension for the good report of the ancient learning of India.

GRANTS OF LAND.

Moreover, in commemoration of his Durbar and as a reward for conspicuous public service, certain grants of land free of revenue, tenable for the life of the grantee or in the discretion of the Local Administration for one further life, shall be bestowed or restored in the North-Western Frontier Province and in Beluchistan.

THE INDIAN PRINCES.

In his gracious solicitude for the welfare of His Royal Indian Princes, His Imperial Majesty has commanded me to proclaim that from henceforth no *Nazarana* payments shall be made upon succession to their States, and sundry debts owing to the Government by the non-jurisdictional estates in Kathiawar and Guzerat, and also by the Bhumia Chiefs of Mewar will be cancelled and remitted in the whole or in part, under the orders of the Government of India, and in appreciation of the Imperial Service Troops certain supernumerary appointments in the Order of British India will be made.

RELEASE OF PRISONERS.

In the exercise of his Royal and Imperial clemency and compassion, His Most Excellent Majesty has been graciously pleased to ordain that certain prisoners now suffering the penalty of the Law for crimes and misdemeanours shall be released from imprisonment, that all those civil debtors now in prison whose debts may be small and due not to fraud but to real poverty, shall be discharged, and that their debts shall be paid.

The persons by whom and the terms and conditions on which these grants, concessions and benefactions shall be enjoyed will be hereafter declared.

God save the King-Emperor.

CHEERS FOR THE KING AND QUEEN.

[The Trumpeters blew another fanfare. Major-General Peyton raised his helmet above his head and standing high in his stirrups shouted for three cheers for the King. A thunderous outburst responded and was repeated again and again, and was called for minutes afterwards. The shouting reverberated the Camps and the City, and all Imperial Delhi was made aware that the King had been proclaimed in its midst. The Herald's voice was again lifted, and three vociferous cheers were given for the Queen.

Their Imperial Majesties arose. The procession was re-formed and proceeded to the Durbar shamiana. The trumpets sounded and once more Colonel Sir Henry M'Mahon announced that the Durbar was over.

"GOD SAVE THE KING."

The Massed Bands played the National Anthem, and the entire assembly sang "God Save the King."]

Appendix C.

INAUGURATION OF THE IMPERIAL CAPITAL.

LORD HARDINGE'S SPEECH.

[In begging Their Majesties the King-Emperor and the Queen-Empress, on 15th December 1911, to lay the first stones of the new Imperial Captital of India, Lord Hardinge made a graceful speech in which he disposed of the supposition that he had acted in any way in the matter of the scheme otherwise than as the head of a unanimous Government, the fact being that the whole of the Members of the Executive Council are warmly supporting the new arrangements. Lord Hardinge said :—]

May it please Your Imperial Majesties.—By graciously consenting to lay the first stones of the Imperial Capital to be established at Delhi, Your Imperial Majesties will set a seal upon the announcement made by His Imperial Majesty on the day of the Coronation Durbar, a day which will ever be memorable in the history of India, partly owing to the splendour with which it was celebrated, but much more on account of the fervent demonstration of loyalty which it evoked.

Many Capitals have been inaugurated in the neighbourhood of Delhi, some of which are so ancient that their origin is lost in the mist of antiquity. But none has ever arisen under happier auspices than those which attend the ceremony which Your Imperial Majesties are about to perform, and assuredly none ever held a promise of greater permanence of a prosperous and glorious future.

The decision to remove the Capital of the Government of India from Calcutta was not reached without mature and anxious consideration. Proposals of a similar nature had been fully discussed as long ago as 1868, and ample materials were on record for the formation of a just opinion upon all debatable points. No great change, however beneficial, can be carried out without some sacrifice, without some injury to personal interests, or some offence to local sentiment. Yet, if I may be permitted to speak as Your Imperial Majesties' Governor-General on behalf of myself and my colleagues in Council,

I desire to say that we are confident that there have been few changes so important which have been so much to the interest of the many, that the injury which the few may anticipate will be merely temporary and within no long time will be greatly outweighed by the benefits which will ensue, and that Your Imperial Majesties' decision, taken constitutionally upon the advice of Your Imperial Majesties' Ministers, will, with the concomitant changes which are necessarily involved, result in a vast and progressive improvement in the methods of the Government of the Indian Empire, will put an end to strife and dissension and will usher in an era of general peace and contentment.

We are convinced that the decision could have been taken and announced in no way which would have been provocative of so little discord and debate, or so well calculated to enlist the enthusiastic and loyal support of all classes of Your Imperial Majesties' faithful subjects.

We sincerely trust that the noble city which under God's Providence we hope to rear around the spot where these stones are laid will be worthy of the occasion to which it owes its birth. The stones themselves will for ever remain a monument of Your Imperial Majesties' gracious presence in this ancient seat of civilisation and Empire, and of the momentous decision which was declared and published to Your Imperial Majesties' loyal subjects at this place.

[At the close of his speech, Lord Hardinge announced that the Maharajah of Gwalior had undertaken to provide a statue of His Majesty the King-Emperor to be set up in the Imperial Capital of India in commemoration of the Royal Visit, and of the transfer of the Capital to Delhi.]

Appendix D.

H. M. KING GEORGE'S PROCLAMATION.

[The following Proclamation was read by the Heralds at the Durbar and throughout India on 12th December 1911 :—]

GEORGE, R.I.

Whereas by Our Royal Proclamations bearing date the nineteenth day of July and the seventh day of November in the Year of Our Lord one thousand nine hundred and ten in the First Year of Our Reign, We did publish and declare Our Royal intention, by the Favour and Blessing of Almighty God, to celebrate the Solemnity of Our Royal Coronation upon the twenty-second day of June, one thousand nine hundred and eleven ;

And whereas, by the Favour and Blessing of Almighty God, We were enabled to celebrate the said Solemnity upon Thursday, the 22nd June last ;

And whereas by Our Royal Proclamation bearing date the twenty-second day of March in the Year of Our Lord one thousand nine hundred and eleven in the First Year of Our Reign, We did declare that it was Our wish and desire Ourselves to make known to all Our loving Subjects within Our Indian Dominions that the said Solemnity had so been celebrated, and to call to Our Presence Our Governors, Lieutenant-Governors, and other of Our Officers, the Princes, Chiefs, and Nobles of the Native States under Our Protection, and the Representatives of all the Provinces of Our Indian Empire;

Now We do, by this Our Royal Proclamation, make announcement thereof and extend to all Our Officers, and to all Princes, Chiefs and Peoples now at Delhi assembled Our Royal and Imperial greeting and assure them of the deep affection with which We regard Our Indian Empire, the welfare and prosperity of which are and ever will be Our constant concern.

Given at Our Court at Delhi, the twelfth day of December, one thousand nine hundred and eleven, in the Second Year of Our Reign.

GOD SAVE THE KING-EMPEROR.

Appendix E.

QUEEN VICTORIA'S PROCLAMATION.

[The following Proclamation was issued on 1st November 1858, after the events of the Mutiny, by Queen Victoria :—]

" Proclamation by the Queen in Council to the Princes, Chiefs and Peoples of India :—

" Victoria, by the Grace of God, of the United Kingdom of Great Britain and Ireland of the Colonies and Dependencies thereof in Europe, Asia, Africa, America and Australia, Queen, Defender of the Faith.

" Whereas, for diverse weighty reasons, We have resolved by and with the advice and consent of the Lords, Spiritual and Temporal, and Commons, in Parliament assembled, to take upon Ourselves the Government of the Territories in India heretofore administered in trust for us by the Honourable East India Company.

" Now therefore, We do by these Presents notify and declare that, by the advice and consent aforesaid, We have taken upon Ourselves the said

To Face Page xvii.

QUEEN VICTORIA.

KING EDWARD VII.

Government; and We hereby call upon all Our Subjects within the said Territories to be faithful, and to bear true Allegiance to Us, Our heirs and successors and to submit themselves to the authority of those whom We may, hereafter from time to time, see fit to appoint to administer the Government of Our said Territories, in our name and on Our behalf.

"We hereby announce to the Native Princes of India that all Treaties and Engagements made with them by or under the authority of the Hon'ble East India Company are by us accepted, and will be scrupulously maintained and We look for the like observance on their part.

"We desire no extension of Our Present territorial Possessions; and while We will permit no aggression upon Our Dominions of Our Rights to be attempted with impunity, We shall sanction no encroachment on those of others. We will respect the Rights, Dignity and Honor of Native Princes as Our own; and We desire that they as well as Our own Subjects, should enjoy that Prosperity and that social advancement which can only be secured by internal Peace and Good Government.

"We hold Ourselves bound to the Natives of Our Indian territories by the same Obligations of Duty which bind Us to all Our other Subjects; and these Obligations, by the Blessing of Almighty God, We shall faithfully and conscientiously fulfil.

"Firmly relying Ourselves on the truth of Christianity, and acknowledging with gratitude the solace of Religion, We disclaim alike the Right and the Desire to impose Our Conviction on any of Our Subjects. We declare it to be Our Royal Will and Pleasure that none be in anywise favoured, none molested or disquieted, by reason of their Religious Faith or Observances, but that all shall alike enjoy the equal and impartial protection of the Law; and We do strictly charge and enjoin all those who may be in authority under Us that they abstain from all interference with the Religious Belief or Worship of Our Subjects, on pain of Our highest Displeasure.

"And it is Our further Will that so far as may be, Our Subjects, of whatever Race or Creed, be free, and impartially admitted to offices in Our Service, the duties of which they may be qualified by their education, ability, and integrity, duly to discharge.

"We know, and respect, the feelings of attachment with which the Native States of India regard the Lands inherited by them from their Ancestors: and We desire to protect them in all Rights connected therewith subject to the equitable demands of the State, and We will that generally in framing and administering the Law, due regard be paid to the ancient Rights, Usages and Customs of India.

"When, by the Blessing of the Providence, internal Tranquillity shall be restored, it is Our earnest Desire to stimulate the peaceful Industry of India, to promote Works of Public Utility and Improvement, and to administer its Government for the benefit of all Our Subjects resident therein. In their prosperity will be Our Strength, in their contentment Our Security and in their gratitude Our Best Reward.

"And may the God of all power grant to us and to those in authority under Us, Strength to carry out these Our Wishes for the good of Our People."

Appendix F.

KING EDWARD VII'S PROCLAMATION.

[The following Proclamation was issued by King Edward VII, on the occasion of the fifth anniversary of Queen Victoria's Proclamation of 1858, on 1st November 1908 :—]

"It is now fifty years since Queen Victoria, my Beloved Mother and my August Predecessor on the Throne of these realms, for diverse weighty reasons, with the advice and consent of Parliament, took upon herself the Government of the territories theretofore administered by the East India Company. I deem this a fitting anniversary on which to greet the Princes and Peoples of India in commemoration of the exalted task then solemnly undertaken.

"Half a century is but a brief span in your long annals yet this half century that ends to-day will stand amid the floods of your historic ages a far-shining landmark. The proclamation of the direct supremacy of the Crown sealed the unity of Indian Government and opened a new era. The journey was arduous and the advance may have sometimes seemed slow, but the incorporation of many strangely diversified communities and of some three hundred millions of the human race under British guidance and control has proceeded steadfastly and without a pause.

"We survey our labours of the past century with a clear gaze and a good conscience.

"Difficulties such as attend all human rule in every age and place have risen up from day to day. They have been faced by the servants of the British Crown with toil and courage and patience with deep counsel and a resolution that has never faltered nor shaken.

"Errors have occurred; the agents of my Government have spared no pains and no self-sacrifice to correct them. If abuses have been proved, vigorous hands have laboured to apply a remedy.

"No secret of Empire can avert the scourge of drought and plague, but experienced administrators have done all that skill and devotion are capable of doing to mitigate those dire calamities of Nature.

"For a longer period than was ever known in your land before, you have escaped the dire calamities of war within your borders, internal peace has been unbroken.

"In the great Charter of 1858 Queen Victoria gave you a noble assurance of her earnest desire to stimulate the peaceful industry of India, to promote works of public utility and improvement and to administer the Government for the benefit of all resident therein.

"The schemes that have been diligently framed and executed for promoting your material convenience and advance—schemes unsurpassed in their magnitude and their boldness—bear witness before the world to the zeal with which that benignant promise has been fulfilled.

"The rights and privileges of the Feudatory Princes and Ruling Chiefs have been respected, preserved and guarded, and the loyalty of their allegiance has been unswerving.

"No man among my subjects has been favoured, molested or disquieted by reason of his religious belief or worship. All men have enjoyed the protection of the Law. The law itself has been administered without disrespect to creed, or caste or to usages and ideas rooted in your civilisation; it has been simplified in form and its machinery adjusted to the requirements of ancient communities slowly entering a new world.

"The charge confided to my Government concerns the destinies of countless multitudes of men, and for ages to come, and it is a paramount duty to repress with a stern arm guilty conspiracies that have no just cause and no serious aim. These conspiracies I know to be abhorrent to the loyal and faithful characters of the vast hosts of my Indian subjects and I will not suffer them to turn me aside from my task of building up the fabric of security and order.

"Unwilling that this historic anniversary should pass without some signal mark of Royal clemency and grace, I have directed that, as was ordered on the memorable occasion of the Coronation Durbar in 1903, the sentences of persons whom our Courts have duly punished for offences against the Law should be remitted or in various degrees reduced and it is my wish that such wrong-doers may remain mindful of this act of mercy and may conduct themselves without offence henceforth.

" Steps are being continuously taken forwards obliterating distinctions of race as the test for access to posts of public authority and power. In this path I confidently expect and intend the progress henceforward to be steadfast and sure, as education spreads, experience ripens and the lessons of responsibility are well learned by the keen intelligence and apt capabilities of India.

" From the first the principle of representative institutions began to be gradually introduced and the time has come when, in the judgment of my Viceroy and Governor-General and others of my counsellors, that principle may be prudently extended.

" Important classes among you, representing ideas that have been fostered and encouraged by British rule, claim equality of citizenship and a greater share in the legislation and Government. The politic satisfaction of such a claim will strengthen, not impair, existing authority and power. The administration will be all the more efficient if the officers who conduct it have greater opportunities of regular contact with those whom it affects and with those who influence and reflect the common opinion about it.

"I will not speak of the measures, that are now being diligently framed for these objects. They will speedily be made known to you and will, I am very confident, mark a notable stage in the beneficent progress of your affairs.

"I recognise the valour and fidelity of my Indian troops and at the New Year I have ordered that opportunity should be taken to show in substantial form this my high appreciation of their martial instincts, their splendid discipline and their faithful readiness for service.

"The welfare of India was one of the objects dearest to the heart of Queen Victoria. By me ever since my visit in 1875, the interests of India, its princes and peoples have been watched with an affectionate solicitude that time cannot weaken. My dear son, the Prince of Wales, and the Princess of Wales, returned from their sojourn among you with warm attachment to your land and true and earnest interest in its well-being and contentment.

"These sincere feelings of active sympathy and hope for India on the part of my Royal House and line only represent, and they do most truly represent, the deep and united will and purpose of the people of this Kingdom.

"May divine protection and favour strengthen the wisdom and mutual good will that are needed for the achievement of a task as glorious as was ever committed to rulers and subjects in any State or Empire of recorded time."

Appendix G.

QUEEN VICTORIA'S MESSAGE TO THE DURBAR OF 1877.

PRINCES AND PEOPLE OF INDIA,—It is now my pleasing duty to communicate to you the gracious message which the Queen, your Empress ; has to-day addressed to you in Her own Royal and Imperial name. These are the words of the telegraphic message which I have this morning received from Her Majesty :

" WE, VICTORIA BY THE GRACE OF GOD, of the United Kingdom, Queen, Empress of India, send through Our Viceroy to all Our officers, Civil and Military, and to all Princes, Chiefs and Peoples now at Delhi assembled, Our Royal and Imperial Greeting, and assure them of the deep interest and earnest affection with which We regard the people of Our Indian Empire. We have witnessed with heartfelt satisfaction the reception which they have accorded to Our beloved Son, and have been touched by the evidence of their loyalty and attachment to Our House and Throne. We trust that the present occasion may tend to unite in bonds of yet closer affection ourselves and our subjects; that from the highest to the humblest all may feel that under Our rule the great principles of liberty, equity, and justice are secured to them; and that to promote their happiness, to add to their prosperity and advance their welfare, are the ever-present aims and objects of Our Empire."

Appendix H.

KING EDWARD'S MESSAGE TO THE DURBAR OF 1903.

" It gives me much pleasure to send a Message of greeting to my Indian people, on the solemn occasion when they are celebrating my Coronation. Only a small number of the Indian Princes and representatives were able to be present at the Ceremony which took place in London; and I accordingly instructed my Viceroy and Governor-General to hold a great Durbar at Delhi, in order to afford an opportunity to all the Indian Princes, Chiefs, and Peoples, and to the Officials of my Government, to commemorate this auspicious event. Ever since my visit to India in 1875, I have regarded that Country and its Peoples with deep affection; and I am conscious of their earnest and loyal devotion to my House and Throne. During recent years many evidences of their attachment have reached me: and my Indian

Troops have rendered conspicuous services in the Wars and Victories of my Empire.

"I confidently hope that my beloved Son, the Prince of Wales, and the Princess of Wales, may before long be able to make themselves personally acquainted with India, a country which I have always desired that they should see, and which they are equally anxious to visit. Gladly would I have come to India upon this eventful occasion myself had this been found possible. I have, however, sent my dear Brother, the Duke of Connaught, who is already so well known in India, in order that my Family may be represented at the Ceremony held to celebrate my Coronation.

"My desire, since I succeeded to the Throne of my revered Mother, the late Queen Victoria, the First Empress of India, has been to maintain unimpaired the same principles of humane and equitable Administration which secured for her in so wonderful a degree the veneration and affection of her Indian Subjects. To all my Feudatories and Subjects throughout India, I renew the assurance of my regard for their liberties, of respect for their dignities and rights, of interest in their advancement, and of devotion to their welfare, which are the supreme aim and object of my rule, and which, under the blessing of Almighty God, will lead to the increasing prosperity of my Indian Empire, and the greater happiness of its People."

Appendix I.

KING GEORGE'S REPLY TO THE MUTINY VETERANS.

[The following is His Majesty's reply to the Mutiny veterans' welcome:—]

King-Emperor's Camp, India,

11th December, 1911.

Dear Sir,

The King-Emperor and the Queen-Empress were much pleased to receive the address from the Indian Mutiny veterans forwarded by you on their behalf. The sight of so many old veterans on parade to-day was for Their Imperial Majesties a most touching scene, for they were looking into the faces and speaking to those who in a time of sore distress stood loyal to their Queen and country and were ready to sacrifice their own lives in defence of that sacred trust. Please assure these old veterans and soldiers of Queen Victoria and King Edward, that they will never be forgotten by their present King-Emperor, who with Her Imperial Majesty, will ever pray their declining years may be spent in peace and happiness.

Believe me,

Yours truly,

(Signed) Stamfordham.

To Major-General A. S. Hunter.